WILDEST
ALASKA

Also by Philip L. Fradkin

———

CALIFORNIA, THE GOLDEN COAST

A RIVER NO MORE

SAGEBRUSH COUNTRY

FALLOUT

WANDERINGS OF AN
ENVIRONMENTAL JOURNALIST

THE SEVEN STATES OF CALIFORNIA

MAGNITUDE 8

WILDEST

ALASKA

JOURNEYS OF GREAT PERIL
IN LITUYA BAY

PHILIP L. FRADKIN

University of California Press
Berkeley   Los Angeles   London

THE FAIRWEATHER RANGE TOWERS ABOVE LITUYA BAY.
The dark, squat shape of Cenotaph Island appears in the foreground.
To the right, above the lone fishing boat, is the bare ridge that was swept
to the 1,740-foot level by the giant wave of 1958. (Photo © 1966, 1967
by Dave Bohn. First reproduced in Glacier Bay: The Land and
the Silence *[San Francisco: Sierra Club, 1967].)*

TITLE PAGE ILLUSTRATION: William Dall, sketch of the entrance to Lituya Bay.

University of California Press
Berkeley and Los Angeles, California

University of California Press, Ltd.
London, England

© 2001 by Philip L. Fradkin

Library of Congress Cataloging-in-Publication Data

Fradkin, Philip L.
    Wildest Alaska : journeys of great peril in Lituya Bay / Philip L. Fradkin.
        p.   cm.
    Includes bibliographical references and index.
    ISBN 0-520-22467-1 (cloth : alk. paper)
        1. Lituya Bay Region (Alaska)—History.   2. Natural history—Alaska—
    Lituya Bay Region.   3. Natural disasters—Alaska—Lituya Bay Region—History.
    4. Violence—Alaska—Lituya Bay Region—History.   5. Fradkin,
    Philip L.—Journeys—Alaska—Lituya Bay Region.   I. Title.
    F912.L57 F73 2001
    979.8'2—dc21

                                                        00-066630

Printed in the United States of America
08 07 06 05 04 03 02 01 00
10 9 8 7 6 5 4 3 2 1

FOR DORIS OBER

*There is always something a bit
over the mark, in sea yarns. Should be.*

D. H. LAWRENCE
ON *MOBY DICK*

─────────

*These are the true names of the places—but why it
has been thought necessary to name them at all, is more
than either you or I can understand. Do you hear any
thing? Do you see any change in the water?*

EDGAR ALLAN POE
"A DESCENT INTO THE MAELSTRÖM"

Contents.

PROLOGUE.

DON MILLER WAS on a U.S. Geological Survey vessel the night of July 9, 1958, when a strong earthquake shook Glacier Bay. Since earthquakes were not that unusual in Southeast Alaska and the damage in the immediate vicinity was minimal, Miller did not react until he heard on the radio early the next morning that some boats had been swamped and people drowned in Lituya Bay.

The geologist had spent time in the remote bay on the Gulf of Alaska coast and had noticed the varying treelines, which suggested massive disturbances in the past. He wondered what had occurred this time.

A plane was quickly chartered. Miller and the pilot departed at 9:15 A.M. that same morning for Lituya Bay, a sixty-mile flight over the towering Fairweather Range. They dropped down to the coast at the point where the La Perouse Glacier disgorges its ice directly into the gulf, then turned north.

Five miles south of the bay large rafts of severed tree trunks were floating on the surface of the water. The freshly denuded trees had been stripped clean of branches and bark and resembled the naked victims of a genocidal act of nature.

As the plane swung right and approached the bay from the gulf, Miller and the pilot could not believe what they saw.

The bay is a shambles, the destruction is unbelievable, Miller hurriedly jotted in his field notebook.

Using the altimeter, they judged the maximum height of the wave that had swept the bay from *the mountains to the sea* at 1,800 feet above sea level. That figure was later adjusted to 1,740 feet, which is 257 feet higher than the world's tallest skyscraper, currently the Petronas Towers in Kuala Lumpur, Malaysia.[†]

There was a fresh scar, and rocks were still falling from the flank of a mountain directly across the inlet. The nearby sea-level snout of the thick Lituya Glacier had been shortened by a quarter mile. Where there had been dense forest along the shoreline the day before, all was now bare rock. The surrounding hills bled. Rivulets of salt water seeped back into the ice- and log-choked bay.

Miller marveled at the tremendous power of the giant wave: "Cut a channel across the top of Cenotaph Island, washed away the cabin there, stripped entire La Chaussee Spit bare, removed lighthouse and several hundred feet of trees adjacent to it at Harbor Point. Washed into Fish Lake to north and across to sea east of The Paps."

Those names and places summoned to mind other water-related tragedies that had contributed to the mournful history of the bay. They dated back to before the first written account in 1786.

The two astonished men flew back and forth over the seven-mile length of the bay for an hour and a half looking for the cause of the miracle of destruction.

[†]The wave was 300 feet higher than the Sears Tower in Chicago, the second tallest building in the world, and it would have cleared the Empire State Building in New York City with 500 feet to spare.

LITUYA BAY JUST BEFORE THE 1958 GIANT WAVE.
(Photo by Don Miller, U.S. Geological Survey.)

LITUYA GLACIER COVERS DESOLATION VALLEY, *the surface manifestation of the Fairweather Fault, in the center. The scooped-out mountainside is on the right. The giant wave bounced off the ridge to the left and rolled out to sea, sweeping along everything in its path, including three fishing boats. (Photo by Don Miller, U.S. Geological Survey.)*

THE WORLD'S HIGHEST KNOWN WAVE—*taller than the tallest skyscraper—decapitated the snout of Lituya Glacier and completely denuded the south end of the ridge to the 1,740-foot level, leaving gleaming rock and a new tree line. (Photo by Don Miller, U.S. Geological Survey.)*

TALL TREES WERE SNAPPED OFF *at root level like so many toothpicks.*
(Photo by Don Miller, U.S. Geological Survey.)

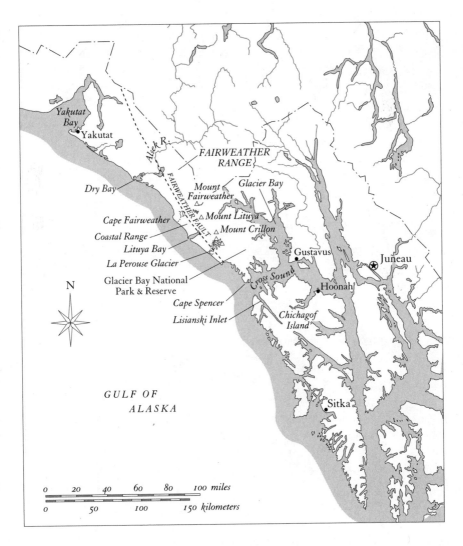

Yakutat
Bay
• Yakutat

Aleck R.

FAIRWEATHER
RANGE

Dry Bay

Mount
Fairweather

Glacier Bay

FAIRWEATHER FAULT

△ Mount Lituya

Cape Fairweather

△ Mount Crillon

Coastal Range

Lituya Bay

• Gustavus

La Perouse Glacier

Cross Sound

Juneau

Glacier Bay National
Park & Reserve

• Hoonah

N

Cape Spencer

Chichagof
Island

Lisianski Inlet

GULF OF
ALASKA

• Sitka

0   20   40   60   80   100 miles

0   50   100   150 kilometers

SOUTHEAST ALASKA

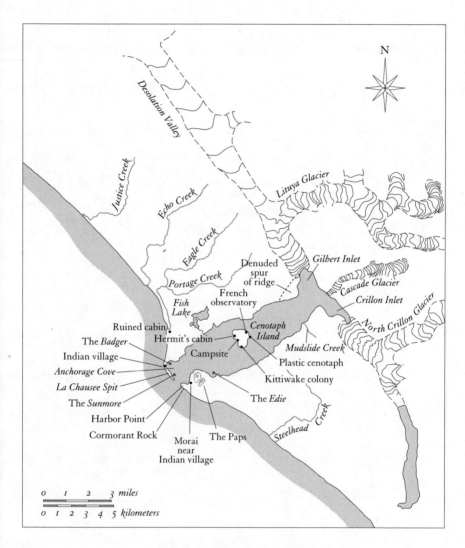

LITUYA BAY AND ITS ENVIRONS

CHAPTER I.

BEGINNINGS.

———

I TOOK MY YOUNG SON ALEX to Alaska for two months during the bicentennial summer of 1976. The idea was for a divorced
father to spend some quality time with his son in a wilderness
setting. In the back of my four-wheel-drive vehicle, in which we
braved heavy traffic on unpaved roads during the peak of pipe-
line construction, were a two-person kayak and paddles neatly
stored in three bags. We unpacked the bags, assembled the kayak,
and paddled in rivers, lakes, and eventually Glacier Bay.

The sightseeing boat took us to the head of the bay, where we
launched the kayak and began a leisurely five-day return trip.
We paddled near glaciers and icebergs, passed through pods of
whales, and celebrated Alex's tenth birthday with a flaming
match stuck in chocolate pudding. Alex hunted for notes hidden
about the tent that described the presents awaiting him in the car
on our return to Juneau.

It was wet and cold, but we managed to stay comfortable.
Grizzly bears and wolves were about on land. On water we felt
vastly superior to the tourists aboard the huge cruise ships, who
watched the scenery on closed-circuit television monitors.

My involvement with Lituya Bay began with the purchase of a
book at the visitor center upon our safe return. It was titled *Glacier Bay: The Land and the Silence* and was written and photo-

graphed by Dave Bohn. The conservationist David Brower had noted in the preface: "Every now and then a man steps onto a landscape and stubs his toe, violently, on the wonder of it all."

I shelved the book on my return home and didn't take it down for another year or so. One winter night I retrieved it and sat by the wood stove. There was a storm outside. Strong gusts of wind pushed the smoke down the chimney and into the living room, where it gathered against the ceiling with the same density as the fog that rolled in from the nearby Pacific Ocean.

I was immediately captured by Bohn's book, or, more precisely, by the first chapter. It dealt with Lituya Bay, a small portion of Glacier Bay National Park far removed from the more accessible inner bay that attracts most airborne visitors and cruise ships. The chapter consisted of eleven pages of text, footnotes, photographs, and other illustrations.

The text began with the sightings of the Alaska coast in 1741 by Russians and went on to relate their misfortunes. It mentioned the offshore passage of the English expedition under Captain James Cook in 1778, recounted the Tlingit Indian legend of the coming of the French in 1786, and described the fate of twenty-one sailors and officers under the command of Jean-François de Galaup, comte de Lapérouse.[†]

This was followed by briefer accounts of subsequent events: the arrival of the Americans in the mid-nineteenth century, the

---

[†]Tlingit is most commonly pronounced "Klink-kit." In formal references, official records, and geographic nomenclature, it is La Pérouse or La Perouse, but the naval officer and explorer signed his name Lapérouse. I have opted for Lapérouse, except for geographic designations.

murder and the lynching at the turn of the century, the time of the hermit, and the giant waves that scoured the heights inside the bay at periodic intervals. Lesser waves intermittently claimed victims at the bay's entrance.

Bohn wrote: "Lituya Bay, wild and incomparable, the thread of violence."

An accomplished photographer, Bohn had selected the illustrations with care. A frontispiece shows Mount Fairweather and the other saw-toothed peaks towering above the snow-clad coastal hills immediately surrounding the bay. Cenotaph Island is a black, squat presence in the middle of the bay. Just to the right of the island is a tiny fishing boat, dwarfed by the immensity of the scene. The boat faces toward the end of the bay and the ridge that was stripped of its thick growth of vegetation by the 1958 wave. When I visited the bay twenty-two years later, the difference between old and new growth along the shoreline was clearly visible.

The other illustration that I found riveting was an engraving rendered in the overwrought European style used to depict the western half of the North American continent in the late eighteenth and nineteenth centuries. Balance is indicated where there is none. In the foreground, two small boats are in the process of capsizing in the tumultuous waves at the entrance to the bay; the masts of two anchored ships peek above the island; two obscure figures, possibly Tlingits, gaze upon the scene from a rock.

I ask: Who would not be caught by this powerful place? How and why were people maimed and destroyed by it?

I don't know the answers to these questions, and I suspect they are the wrong ones to ask. Perhaps there is no need for questions, just the necessity to experience such a compelling landscape, at least once in a lifetime.

What is clear, however, is that the bay is an excellent laboratory in which to study the power of a place. It is a singular power and a dark place, to be sure—definitely not a glowing mountain, a meandering stream, or a canyon wilderness, the types of places usually selected to depict the invigorating and healing aspects of nature.

There is another side to nature, however, one that we ignore at our peril. Over the last forty years I have experienced firsthand the destructive forces of nature in California, be they earthquakes, fires, floods, hurricanes, tornadoes, or tsunamis. To a certain extent these phenomena have shaped our culture, made us who we are, made me who I am. Lituya Bay is a more extreme and isolated example of this shaping process that occurs throughout the world.[†]

California plays a small part in this history and memoir, too. For Lituya Bay is connected to the bay on whose shoreline I have lived since 1977. The line of constant fracturing runs through Lituya Bay and Tomales Bay, just north of San Francisco, and then loops around the world wherever tectonic plates meet to grind the grist that is known as history.

But history, especially of a wild place, is not continuous. There are total blanks and wafer-thin links in the chain of evidence that runs through this Gothic nature tale. What is missing

---

[†]Landscape, or nature, as a factor in determining history and destiny is a theme I also explore in my most recent books, *The Seven States of California: A Natural and Human History* (1995), and *Magnitude 8: Earthquakes and Life Along the San Andreas Fault* (1998).

represents the inadequacies of history and ourselves—what we can't know and what we don't want to know.

I FIND MYSELF constantly edging toward Alaska.

Every Sunday morning, and sometimes during the week, weather and tides permitting, I row upon Tomales Bay. The thick, dripping vegetation on the fog-enshrouded Point Reyes Peninsula, which borders the bay, reminds me of Southeast Alaska. The peninsula is, in fact, advancing toward Alaska with every new seismic displacement.

Tomales Bay is no ordinary body of water. It is the surface manifestation of the San Andreas Fault, which is why it is arrow straight and long and narrow.

Like Lituya Bay in Alaska, Tomales Bay was formed by the tremendous forces that push and pull the earth apart at the ragged margins of the North American and Pacific plates. The two bays lie athwart the Pacific ring of violent movement and fire, that tectonic trough where the huge continental plates are restlessly joined. Their startling movements cause disruptions of greater or lesser magnitudes that work insidiously upon the human psyche.

In terms of direction, I have one choice: to row toward the northwest. The outlet is in that direction. Tomales Bay ends a short distance to the southeast.

Should I row far enough north—assuming that I had the requisite stamina, my skiff was seaworthy, and I was able to portage short distances over land—I would wind up on the Fairweather Fault, which is the crossbar on the T that slices through the terminus of Lituya Bay.

No, I'm not in training for that seismic journey. Rather, I note the connection between the two bays as I dip my oars into the placid water and silently glide past curious seals, startled loons, and other migrating waterfowl who are on their way either north or south, depending upon the season.

The rhythmic pull on the oars is hypnotic, and my mind dwells upon the commonalties of place.

Both bays have treacherous waves at their narrow entrances; both have a single island in their midst; both are surrounded by varying degrees of heights; both are contained within units of the national park system; and both have had recent seismic spasms, the two tectonic plates pulling twenty feet apart in 1906 in Tomales Bay and an equivalent distance in Lituya Bay in 1958. As a result, both are known as earthquake bays.

Others, more scientifically inclined than I, have commented on the similarities.

Don Tocher, a seismologist at the University of California at Berkeley who edited the *Bulletin of the Seismological Society of America,* visited both bays. He noted in that publication: "The physiography of this valley [Desolation Valley] in the Fairweather fault zone is similar in many respects to that of the trough in the San Andreas fault zone between Tomales and Bolinas bays in California."[†]

So far, I have not had to row for my life in Tomales Bay, as the Frenchmen did in that other bay more than two hundred years

[†]Ron Redfern documents the similarities between Lituya and Tomales bays, using words and photographs, in *The Making of a Continent* (1986), which was the basis for a PBS series.

ago. There is always that possibility, however, given the strong winds that rise suddenly and the periodic sneaker waves that crash upon the bar at the mouth of Tomales Bay.

I don't know what all this means, other than the fact that somehow these two places are yoked together, and I have been drawn to both and fused to each.

CHAPTER II

THE P *LACE*.

———

LITUYA BAY, the principal character in this tale, is compelling for its deadly beauty.

It is surrounded by a wildly spectacular and volatile landscape, whose history has been punctuated by the grinding action of the glacial ice that rapidly advances and retreats across its surface; by destructive earthquakes; by freakish giant waves that move with blinding speed toward the gulf; and by other lethal waves that unexpectedly burst upon its entrance from the opposite direction. The glaciers have scraped the landscape to bare bone, the earthquakes have toppled mountains, and the waves have periodically decimated the vegetation and a large percentage of the few people who, since the time of the Tlingits, have infrequently visited the bay.

Like an island, Lituya Bay is a separate place. It is walled off by mountains and the Gulf of Alaska from the outside world. The only access is by small boat or seaplane; and when it storms or when the fog closes in and the waves build up at the entrance, that place is locked up tighter than a concrete crypt.

Juneau, the state capital and nearest small city, is one hundred and twenty miles to the east. Yakutat, the nearest village, is one hundred miles to the northwest. To the west is the Gulf of Alaska, one of the wildest bodies of water in the world. Fierce, rain-whipped gales from off the gulf, clumped together in successive series of four or five, can close down the coast for weeks at a time. Screaming winds are at their strongest in the late fall and early winter months, with gusts regularly approaching or exceeding hurricane speeds. Violent squalls, known as williwaws, unexpectedly swoop down mountain slopes and rake exposed anchorages. There is fog year-round; and even if there is no fog, most days are cloudy.

One of the best descriptions of the liquid aspect of this region is contained in the novel *The Sea Runners*. Ivan Doig observes: "Vaster stretches can be found on the earth, but not all so many, and none as fiercely changeable. . . . Within this water world the special law of gravity is lateral and violent. Currents of brine and air rule."

Ice is a barrier on the other three sides of Lituya Bay.

Cutting off access on the north is the outfall of the Fairweather Glacier, and on the south is the La Perouse Glacier, an even more impenetrable barrier. Ice from the latter glacier spills directly into the gulf, making it the only glacier in Alaska to disgorge its contents directly into the open water.

To the east, toward the populated areas of Southeast Alaska, there are three barriers. First, there is the three-thousand-foot Coastal Range. Then there is the rubble and glacier-strewn gutter of Desolation Valley—the surface manifestation of the Fairweather Fault.

Towering above all are the frozen wastelands of the Fairweather Range, whose highest peak is over fifteen thousand feet. This range is the southeastern extension of the Saint Elias Mountains. Nowhere else in the world do mountains tower so far above the ocean. The second and fourth highest peaks in North America lie within this region, as well as a dozen other mountains that are higher than the highest mountain in the lower forty-eight states.[†]

This is not a still place. There have been nine major earthquakes since 1899. Because of frequent violent movements along the fault lines, the mountains are rising rapidly—forty-seven feet in the 1899 earthquake and fifty feet in 1958.

FROM EARLIEST TIMES, Lituya Bay has encouraged animism.

I see the T-shaped bay as a maddened mother-whale attempting to tear herself from the grip of the land. Her flukes are grasped by the stone mountains that rise abruptly from the head of the bay, her open mouth is the narrow outlet to the sea, her teeth are the rocks at the entrance, and Cenotaph Island is her single bloated eye. Despite her strenuous efforts, the leviathan is trapped forever within this rock-ribbed cage. Her frantic thrashings cause the unusual waves.

Names and dimensions have been attached to this crazed mammalian presence over the years. The flukes, which span three miles, are Gilbert Inlet to the north and Crillon Inlet to the south. Snaking down from the mountains above, Lituya Glacier empties into Gilbert Inlet, and North Crillon Glacier spills into the inlet of the same name. Splitting them is Cascade Glacier, which drops directly into the center of the tail.

The whale's body extends east and west for a distance of seven miles and has a width varying from three-fourths of a mile to

---

[†] The second and fourth highest peaks are Mount Logan, 19,524 feet, and Mount Saint Elias, 18,008 feet. Mount McKinley, or Denali, 20,320 feet, is the highest peak in North America. Mount Whitney in California, at 14,494 feet, is the highest mountain in the contiguous states.

two miles.[†] The jaw juts one mile into the gulf and the overlapping upper lip is La Chaussee Spit, nearly one mile long and five hundred feet wide, with a maximum elevation of twelve feet. The spit, a terminal moraine, marks the furthest advance of the most recent glacier three to four hundred years ago.[‡]

Harbor Point anchors the lower jaw. Cormorant Rock, just off the point, and two nearby rocks are the sharp incisors, which have ripped the hulls of a significant number of vessels over the years. The navigable portion of the mouth is one hundred and fifty feet wide.

The glacially scoured bay reaches a maximum depth of seven hundred and twenty feet, enough for the occasional whale seen swimming within it. The heights immediately surrounding the fjord-like bay rise steeply to between two thousand and six thousand feet.

There is a maximum tidal range of fifteen feet. With such a tremendous volume of water pouring in and out twice during a twenty-four-hour period, currents at the constricted entrance reach speeds of nearly fifteen miles per hour. Treacherous waves can form instantaneously on an ebb (outgoing) tide, particularly when an opposing wind blows from the gulf.

When the *U.S. Coast Pilot,* the navigator's bible, employed more descriptive language, this was the warning issued for the entrance to the bay:

[†]More accurately, the orientation for the body is approximately northeast-southwest and for the flukes northwest-southeast, but I have simplified it for storytelling purposes.

[‡]Chaussée, a name bestowed by the French, means embankment or causeway. It appears as Chaussee on maps and charts.

The ebb currents, running out against a southwest swell, cause bad topping seas or combers across the entire entrance, through which no small boat could live. Small-powered vessels inside the bay should keep away from the entrance on the ebb to avoid being swept through. The ebb current flows in a narrow stream for several miles out to sea, and can be seen at a distance of several miles, forming a prominent mark for the entrance. On the flood the entrance is smooth, and with a calm sea local fishing boats often enter, being quickly swept through the center of the channel by the powerful current. However, no stranger should attempt to enter except at slack water. Slack water lasts from 10 to 20 minutes.

That deadly waves emanate from the land as well is a function of the surrounding mountains' great heights, the deep water of the bay, and periodic seismic disturbances, which loosen huge amounts of rocks and ice and pitch them directly into the bay, thus causing a massive displacement of water. The immediate results are great splash waves that decimate vegetation, wildlife, and any humans unfortunate enough to be found in their paths as they ricochet wildly toward the sea.

The North Pacific, and the Gulf of Alaska in particular, has the most fearsome waves in the world. The giant wave of 1958 that reached a height of 1,740 feet was a world's record.[†] The second highest wave was also recorded in the gulf. A wind-whipped wave encountered in the open sea north of Hawaii reached a height of 112 feet, as measured on board the USS *Ramapo* on February 7, 1933.

[†] For official recordkeeping purposes, types of waves are not differentiated.

Inland from the coast the dark-green interior is virtually inaccessible. It is guarded by a dense rain forest consisting of interlocking trees, thick shrubs, and the spikes of devil's club plants. The vegetation, swamps, and coastal streams are fed by more than one hundred inches of rainfall annually.

It is an outsized land dominated by water in all its forms: glacial ice, snow, and rain; rivulets, streams, creeks, and rivers; fogs, mists, vapors, and low clouds. There are bogs, swamps, ponds, peatlands, heaths, and muskeg. In the dark fall and winter months there are frequent gales. Snow drifts pile up in the lowland forest of Sitka spruce and western hemlock that shades into Alaska yellow cedar and mountain hemlock on the hillsides.

Lituya Bay is an easier place for the abundant wildlife than for humans. Black and grizzly bears roam with ease through the forests and up onto the lower reaches of the mountains. Their tracks and scat can be seen everywhere. Bear trails are one way to get around in the dense undergrowth. Gray wolves travel in packs across the open hillsides. Mountain goats live on Billy Goat Ridge and elsewhere.

There is a teeming bird population, the bay being a major stop on the Pacific Flyway. On a bare cliff on the south side of Cenotaph Island there is a resident colony of some three thousand black-legged kittiwakes. Bald eagles, peregrine falcons, and ravens prey upon the colony, as do humans with guns. At such times, or shortly before an earthquake, the white gulls sound their raucous alarm cry of *kittiwake, kittiwake, kittiwake* and scatter to the nearby black sand beaches.

HUMANS HAVE EXPERIENCED this place and testified to its power, some with their lives. More, perhaps many more, than two hundred people have drowned within the narrow entrance and the enclosed bay. An exact determination of the number of deaths is impossible, given the vagaries of recordkeeping over thousands of years in this isolated region.

The Tlingits thought of Lituya Bay as a bad place. They had no expression to describe blue skies, but plenty of words covered stormy weather. From the time of the Native Americans onward, people clung only intermittently to the edges of this hostile land, where the magnetic compass variations are extreme.

The French came to know it similarly, as did others who followed in their wake. One such person was George T. Emmons, an American naval lieutenant and collector of native artifacts who served on board two patrol vessels that plied the gulf coast during the late nineteenth century—the time of greatest usage of the bay. Emmons wrote: "Originally the bed of a great glacier, it has long since been taken possession of by the sea, that floods and ebbs through its restricted entrance with a force that makes it the most justly feared harbor on the Pacific coast."

The scientist who knew this region best was Don Miller. For Miller, it represented the extremes of wildest Alaska. This was how the geologist described the area shortly before the giant wave of 1958:

The Gulf of Alaska area is one of bold contrasts: within a
short distance, the traveler may experience many extremes of
environment characteristic of the territory; forest and under-
brush as dense as any in the southernmost part of Alaska
adjoining vast ice-covered lands as desolate and more arctic
in appearance than northern Alaska; the fog, heavy rainfall,
dense clouds, violent storms, and uniform temperature of
the Aleutians; the aridity and extremes of summer and win-

ter temperatures characteristic of the upper Yukon Valley. Mount St. Elias, rivaling Mount McKinley in height, towers over a coastal plain that, in part, is as flat and swampy as the Yukon [River] Delta. . . . Within the area lie thousands of square miles of wilderness counted among the least known and least frequented parts of Alaska.

George Plafker was an authority on the Fairweather Fault. A colleague of Miller's, Plafker worked in Lituya Bay in the early 1950s. Some years later he told me: "Knowing what I know now, I get nervous about being there. It is a brooding place with those glaciers, the large masses of rock, and the low clouds. When it is clear, it is one of the most beautiful places in the world. From a geologic point of view, it is a very interesting place. The deformation is quite active."

I have emphasized the violence of the bay. In between cataclysmic events, however, there were periods of tranquillity, which lulled the occasional human visitors into believing that they were in a normal place. A fortunate few—mostly mountain climbers—escaped unscathed.

CHAPTER III.

THE TLINGITS.

————

SOME TWENTY YEARS AGO I visited the Tlingit villages of Angoon and Hoonah, touched down briefly at Yakutat, and spent time at the native corporation headquarters in Juneau. Acceptable prehistory, as we know it, doesn't emanate from a writer talking to such sources or from the unfiltered words of the natives themselves. It comes from professional recorders and interpreters of cultures known as ethnographers.

Ethnography is a branch of anthropology that produces what are considered scientific descriptions of cultures. Most ethnographers are academics who believe they practice objectivity. However, they face the basic problem of how to produce scientific texts based on personal experiences.

Casual travelers, like myself, produce readable texts from archival research and personal experiences. There are, however, similarities. Scholars who have written studies of the Tlingits are, like me, white and middle class and from the lower forty-eight states.[†]

[†]The preeminent ethnographer of the Tlingits was Frederica de Laguna, a professor of anthropology at Bryn Mawr College in Pennsylvania. At the other end of the spectrum from de Laguna's "real as seashell" approach to ethnography is Carlos Castaneda's "sorcerer's apprentice" methodology. There is little agreement among ethnographers on how to document "exotic others."

THE FIRST HUMAN inhabitants of interior Alaska migrated across the Bering land bridge some fifty thousand to fifteen thousand years ago and then, because it took additional time to penetrate the coastal mountain barrier, settled in the protected interior fjords and channels of Southeast Alaska around nine thousand years ago. There they began to establish, as one anthropologist put it, "the spectacular culture of abundance that is famous in the ethnographic literature."

It took even longer for humans to reach the more isolated coast. The earliest inhabitants came on foot along the shoreline, through the Alsek River corridor to Dry Bay, paddled northward from Cross Sound, or drifted eastward on the current from Japan.

Within the last three thousand years, these Paleo-Indians were displaced by the Tlingits, who moved in and out of Lituya Bay in accordance with the seasons and the ebb and flow of the glaciers. The last ice-free period began in the late sixteenth century. The most recent seasonal inhabitants had thus occupied the bay for only two hundred years before the coming of the first Europeans in 1786.

The Tlingits, like the white strangers, had their creation myths involving a flood and an immaculate conception that were rich in metaphor. Raven was to the Tlingits what the trickster Coyote was to the Southwest Indians. The Raven cycle was at the center of their creation stories, and Raven was involved in accounts of natural phenomena, such as earthquakes.

There are countless versions of the Tlingit flood story, depending on which ethnographer heard it from what informant in which year and through what interpreter. What follows is the oldest recorded version, as compiled by the German anthropologist Aurel Krause, using French orthography:

> Kitkh-oughin-si, the first inhabitant of the earth, had several children by his sister whom he killed so that mankind would not multiply. His power extended over all inhabitants of earth and he punished them for their misbehavior by a flood. However he could not destroy them all, because they saved themselves in boats on the tops of mountains where one can still see the remains of the boats and the ropes by which they fastened themselves.[†]
>
> The sister of Kit-ká-ositiyi-qa [*sic*] separated herself during the flood from her cruel brother and along a beach met a large and handsome man, who, when he discovered the reason for her flight, made her swallow a small round stone and promised her that she would bear a son whom nobody could kill. The result of this was the birth of Raven.

Incest and Raven were also associated with earthquakes. The French anthropologist Claude Lévi-Strauss related the following Tlingit story about the movement of the earth:

> An incestuous brother and sister had to part. The brother became the Thunderbird who is responsible for hurricanes and tempests. Once a year, in the stormy season, he comes back to visit his sister. The latter, named Agischanak in the old sources, Hayicanak in more recent ones, went underground at the top of a mountain. Since then, she has supported the column on which the earth rests; she likes hu-

---

[†]The tops of the mountains were identified as the summits of Mount Fairweather and Mount Saint Elias.

mans who make a fire to warm her, because each time she gets hungry, the ground shakes and the humans burn grease to feed her. According to other versions, the quakes occur when she fights off Raven, the trickster, who, to destroy men, jostles her and tries to make her lose her grip on the column supporting the earth.

This story is similar to myths of other indigenous people around the world who attributed earthquakes to a susceptible support system manned by an elder, an animal, or a god.

THE TLINGITS LIVED in an abundant land and revered wealth, social status, and war. In this, they were not unlike the French at the end of the eighteenth century, who were the first Europeans to come into contact with the Lituya Bay Tlingits. There are also clear parallels with the Americans at the beginning of the twenty-first century. Iron, gold, and financial stocks were the coins of the respective realms.

Out of necessity the Tlingits were principally a water-oriented people, with a culture based on the southern arctic tradition. They cultivated tobacco but practiced no other agriculture. They subsisted mainly on fish, sea mammals, and berries. Their only domestic animal was the dog. They lived in groups no larger than one thousand, and often much smaller.

The acquisition of wealth led to leadership and social standing. Wealth was not only received or taken, it was also given in Tlingit society. Wealth given honored a house's dead, since the dead received the spiritual equivalent of the gift.

It was not the accumulation but the circulation of wealth that distinguished the Tlingit culture. To receive and not give was a grave offense; it meant a relationship was severed, a circle broken. Not only the spiritual health of the community depended upon the exchange of wealth, usually during elaborate ceremonies called potlatches, but also its economic well-being.

Communication between the scattered groups among the islands, fjords, and channels of Southeast Alaska was by boat, and they used their slim kayaks and gracefully flared war canoes very skillfully indeed. Their totem poles have become well known, and their animistic masks, lodged in the American Museum of Natural History in New York and elsewhere, greatly influenced the surrealist and abstract expressionist painters of the twentieth century.

Of these masks, Lévi-Strauss said they combined the "contemplative serenity of the statues of Chartres and the Egyptian tombs with the gnashing artifices of Halloween." They were marriages of opposites, like the plumed serpent of the ancient Aztecs. Their void-like, protuberant, or cylindrical eyes represented a penetrating vision.

The Tlingits had a strong sense of territory. The independent clans were the core groups. The many clans within the seventeen geographically determined tribes controlled hunting and fishing grounds, such as Lituya Bay. Power was exercised by the respective clan chiefs and male councils, Lituya Bay first being used by the Yakutat Tlingits and then coming under the seasonal jurisdiction of the Hoonah Tlingits.

Both before and after the first Russians set foot on this coastline in 1741, the different Tlingit factions fought any encroachment on their domains with an unbridled fierceness that others came to fear. Motives for war ranged from the perceived need for revenge, to a desire for slaves and property, to access to hunting and fishing grounds. There were specialized weapons: the slave killer, a moose or sheep horn mounted on a stick that resembled a pick; a braining stone, favored by assassins; iron and copper daggers; ivory or wooden war clubs; spears; bows and crossbows; and, later, firearms.

The long-haired shamans were central to the act of war. Both priest and doctor, since he had the ability to cure, the shaman was consulted on the most propitious time to wage war and on its likely outcome. He replied with suitable Delphic ambiguity. The shaman sent his spirit to spy upon the enemy and to engage the rival shaman's spirit. He also presided over purification rites and abstinence before battle and accompanied the warriors in the large war canoes.

They raided as they went. Heads and scalps, redeemable later by grieving relatives at a price, were taken as trophies by the warriors, who were clad in wooden armor, helmets, and protective masks, all as expertly wrought as the metal armor of medieval knights.

Although mistakes were made in the heat of battle, the Tlingits attempted to avoid drowning their enemies. Death by drowning was the most feared of all deaths, for it could haunt the living. Land Otter Men, the most powerful and feared supernatural beings in the Tlingit cosmology, were associated with such deaths.

The Tlingits believed that following death the individual's spirit passed through a ghostly transition phase before reincarnation amongst living relatives as a newborn child. The absence of a proper cremation ceremony interrupted the cycle. All but the shamans, whose bodies or heads were wrapped in skins and left upon a wooden platform, were cremated. To disturb these remains meant sickness or death.

Given the absence of a drowned body, the soul of a dead person was consigned to the form of a Land Otter Man, who wandered in an eternal abyss. The Tlingit expression for drowning translated to "is captured by Land Otter Men."

Such a spirit, who was closely associated with the occult powers of the shaman, had a human body, long hair, a round mouth, and the tail of a land otter. They lived in dens in the woods, in underwater caverns, or on spits of land, there being an easy interchangeability between land and water for Land Otter Men. They were always referred to as masculine: he appeared and disappeared, he ate raw food, or his voice could be identified by a stutter or a whistle.

To the Tlingits the land otter, whose whistling cry was well known, was transitional, between two worlds, anomalous, and thus unpredictable. The otter lived beyond the limits of society in the wild streams and remote forests bordered by devil's club.

The North American land or river otter, *Lutra canadensis pacifica,* was known as *kucka* to the Tlingits. The ethnologist Frederica de Laguna wrote: "Tlingit mythology is full of tales about these creatures and everyone, myself included, has had some personal experience of a sudden or startling encounter with a land otter."

There were stories of white men encountering Land Otter Men on the outer coast. De Laguna related the following account in her three-volume study of the Tlingits: A big storm struck near Yakutat. Two white men were drowned and another was found barely alive on the beach by a friend in an airplane. The narrator said: "Butch was landed by him and trying to help him up to the plane. Bill refused to go. He saw so many slim mans around him. He saw them himself. Those slim mans were talking excited. That was Land Otter Men."

These spirits were quite prevalent in Lituya Bay, where there had been many drownings.

There were dangers from corporeal animals living in and around the bay as well, and none was greater than the threat posed by the many grizzly or brown bears, with whom the shaman's power, or *yek,* was equated. "They say it looks like a bear, but it grows," said a Tlingit of a shaman's *yek.* "The more tribe you have, the more people in the tribe, the bigger [the *yek*] is."

The bear crest was the emblem of an important kinship group that visited the bay. It was emblazoned on totem poles, stones, hides, faces, garments, and baskets.

There was a duality about the bay. For the Tlingits, Lituya Bay was the most feared place in all their vast territory. But the bay also had the advantages of being a harbor of refuge on an otherwise inaccessible stretch of coast. It offered the defense of distance from enemies and was rich in natural resources.

The Tlingits used the bay as a summer hunting and fishing camp. Their settlements, not all inhabited simultaneously, were grouped around the entrance on both shores. Three hundred of them might be in the bay at one time, with many more coming and going. There were sandy coves, where canoes could be beached, and quick access to the rich offshore fishing grounds, abundant fresh water, firewood, berries, and tranquillity — most of the time.

THEN, WITHOUT WARNING, disaster would strike, and Lituya Bay would become a fearsome place.

Land Otter Men were the principal factors in many of the Tlingits' stories involving the destructive waves that emanated from both ends of Lituya Bay. The particulars of the stories vary, and they are, for the most part, without time elements, thus confounding the western desire for a single, chronological story line.

What follows floats in time.

One day ten canoes belonging to a visiting clan departed from the bay. There were eight men in each canoe. They were either on their way to make war on the Chilkat Tlingits or on a trading expedition.

Before leaving they knew something terrible was going to happen because Mount Fairweather had given a sign.[†]

They killed a bald-headed man and cut his head off at the mouth of Chilkat River. The young warriors got excited; the head was in their way; they threw it overboard. The hairless man was transformed into a hairy Land Otter Man.

Big Raven, the shaman, asked: "Who threw that bald-headed head overboard?" He pointed to each of the young warriors: "You?" "You?" "Was it you?"

To repair this untoward act, they sent one of the warriors to the enemy camp to be killed; but he died on the way of a heart attack.

[†]De Laguna wrote of Mount Fairweather: "Its appearance gives promise of calm seas or warns of storms, and it is therefore called 'the paddlers' mountain by the natives." A Tlingit woman told de Laguna, "But that mountain that they go by—they see something that give them warning. That showed when a storm is coming up. That's the only thing they travel by." White whalers working the offshore Fairweather Grounds in the midnineteenth century believed that when the mountain cleared, several days of good weather would follow.

The shaman of the Chilkat Tlingits, Wild Currents, was angered by the loss of the head, so he upset the boats on their return to Lituya Bay. The Indian source told the ethnographer: "They believe that is the cause of it all, because the bald-headed man was killed. That's why the doctor gets mad at us. It was to make it even he upset the canoes."

There was also a simpler explanation for the drownings: "They were in Lituya Bay for a rest. They struck it at the wrong tide. The big rock got them."

Regardless of the cause, all were lost, including eight brothers. One brother made the sound of a frog as he drowned. A sister, who witnessed the drownings, composed some songs about it. When the water was smooth, she would sit by the entrance to the bay and alternately cry and sing. One song went: "Your grandfathers were watching the paddler's mountain. Close by, your hands miss it."

A third version of the story has the Russians being enticed into the bay by a trail of riches that floated out to sea from the overturned canoes. A Tlingit woman said: "You know that Lituya Bay. Those people drowned over there. And all that good stuff washed out to sea—sea otter skins wash out to sea. And those halibut skin bags, it floats. The Russians get it. That's why the Russians came to Lituya Bay."

Variants of this story told by other Tlingits speak of seven or eight canoes. With a maximum of ten canoes, a minimum of seven, and ten men to a canoe, the death toll would have been between seventy and one hundred, thus making it perhaps the single greatest tragedy in a bay that specialized in that particular genre.

The French arrived just after another mass drowning. In 1886, one hundred years after the French entered Lituya Bay, a Tlingit chief told Lieutenant Emmons the following story: Before the coming of the white man, when the natives had no iron, the Chilkat and Hoonah Tlingits made long canoe trips each summer to Yakutat to trade for copper. One spring a large party under the command of three chiefs headed north. On entering Lituya Bay, four canoes were swallowed by the waves, and all their occupants, including one of the chiefs, were drowned. While the survivors were mourning the loss, two French ships entered the bay.

The Tlingits, through sign language, told the French of the most recent tragedy. In this version, seven canoes were lost. Lapérouse recorded it thus:

> Every day we saw fresh canoes enter the bay; and every day whole villages departed, and gave place to others. These Indians seemed to have considerable dread of the passage, and never ventured to approach it, unless at the slack water of flood or ebb. By the help of our glasses we distinctly perceived, that, when they were between the two points, the chief, or at least the principal Indian, arose, stretched out his arms towards the sun, to which he appeared to address a prayer, while the rest paddled away with all their strength. In the course of our inquiries respecting this custom, we learned, that seven very large canoes had lately been lost in this passage, while an eighth escaped. This [the eighth canoe] the Indians who were saved consecrated to their god, or to the memory of their comrades. We saw it by the side of a [tomb], which no doubt contained the ashes of some who were shipwrecked.

A drawing was made of the eighth canoe by an artist who accompanied the French expedition. It was a large canoe with wooden frames and a skin cover, not like the local dugout canoes. Such canoes could hold twenty men. Given that between four and seven canoes were lost in the combers at the entrance, I would arbitrarily assign fifteen men to each of five canoes, which would yield a death toll of approximately seventy-five. Again being conservative, perhaps one hundred and fifty Tlingits died in these two separate incidents. Other drownings went unrecorded, and thus were lost to history.

The waves became myths communicated in symbolic form.

One legend of the waves at the entrance to the bay was depicted on a carved wooden pipe collected by Emmons. The ten-inch-long pipe was used by the Hoonah Tlingits at important ceremonies, such as to honor the dead.

Squatting at one end of the pipe was a frog with glittering abalone shells for eyes. At the other end a bear slave sat on his haunches. They held the surface of the bay between them and agitated it, much like a blanket being violently tossed. Two triangular prongs represented the waves. Sinking beneath the waves was a copper canoe with two occupants.

The frog, who represented the spirit of Lituya Bay, was also the crest of a clan that intermittently used the bay and a figure in Tlingit mythology that was greatly feared, since it had the same amphibious characteristics as Land Otter Men. The frog captured people and was associated with death.

In the legend that the pipe illustrated, a monster of the deep, known as Kah Lituya, which translated "Man of Lituya," lived in an underwater cavern near the entrance. He resented any intrusion into his domain. A lookout was stationed atop Mount Fairweather. When vessels approached the entrance to the bay, a warning was given, and the frog figure and the bear slave grabbed the surface of the water and violently shook it. Those who entered the bay were seized and made bear slaves.

There were fewer tales concerning the giant waves, perhaps because they were far less frequent. Disrespect shown to Land Otter Men could cause such waves.

The Lituya Bay Tlingits boasted that they were not afraid of things that stuttered or did not speak correctly, characteristics of Land Otter Men. The shaman, who lived along the Alsek River, heard of this blasphemy and predicted that a disaster would befall his neighbors to the south in Lituya Bay.

Soon thereafter two men from Lituya Bay went hunting on a nearby hill and saw a great avalanche or flood descend into the bay. "This flood was caused by an avalanche which poured into [the bay] and filled it up, forcing the water out," according to one version. The hunters returned to their camp and found the bodies of their relatives and friends hanging from the branches of trees. They believed that the massive wave had been caused by angry Land Otter Men.

The Tlingits' perception of the bay was recorded by an ethnographer, who made the following notation concerning his informant: "J. E. says that Lituya Bay is a bad place."

CHAPTER IV

THE FRENCH.

―――――

THE FIRST EUROPEAN ENCOUNTER with Alaska set the precedent for later disappearances and deaths.

Vitus Bering, a Dane in the employ of the Russian czar, and Alexis Chirikov, who commanded the Russian packet boat *Saint Paul,* set off on a voyage of discovery in 1741. They sailed together from Kamchatka in two vessels and then became separated. Chirikov spied land on July 15th, one day before Bering did.

"Thus was the great discovery achieved," wrote Hubert Howe Bancroft in his *History of Alaska.* Chirikov noted in his log: "The land was full of mountains, some covered with snow and all with trees."

Three days later, and somewhere to the northwest, Chirikov sent a boat ashore containing eleven men armed with muskets and a small brass cannon. They were to reconnoiter what seemed like an opening to a bay and were given precise written instructions. They should ascertain who lived there, to whom the land belonged, the size of the population, the form of government, the location of valuable ores, and the nature of the vegetation— all within twenty-four hours. The sailors were to treat the natives kindly and distribute trifling gifts, including ten rubles. On landing, they were to build a large signal fire.

Where exactly did they go ashore? Historians who specialize in the exploration of the Northwest are split on the location.

Some say Lituya Bay and others Lisianski Strait, which lies seventy miles to the south between Yakobi and Chichagof islands. Chirikov's description fits both places.[†]

There was no signal fire. The boat and its crew failed to return. Bad weather obscured the land. The *Saint Paul* wore a path in the sea, sailing on and off shore.

On July 23rd smoke was spotted, as were human figures. All that night a cannon boomed at regular intervals from the mother ship, and a lantern was hung in the rigging.

On July 24th the weather was fair and the sea calm. A second, smaller boat was dispatched with four men aboard, including a carpenter and a caulker. They were to repair the first boat and then return immediately.

The *Saint Paul* sailed close enough to land to see the surf breaking upon the rocks. Again, there was no prearranged signal. The cannon boomed all night; there was a fire on the beach.

The next day two boats could be seen setting out from shore. The Russians sailed hopefully toward them before it was ascertained that the two canoes were filled with natives. The larger canoe hovered protectively in the background. The smaller one approached the eighty-foot vessel.

The four Indians stood and shouted, "Agai, agai." The sailors did not know what to make of such strange noises. (Scholars

---

[†]The American F. A. Golder (1914) first said Lituya and then (1922) Lisianski. The Englishman J. C. Beaglehole (1967), Captain James Cook's biographer and editor of his journals, combined the two separate places into one and then quoted a description of Lituya Bay from the *U.S. Coast Pilot*. Glynn Barratt (1981), a New Zealand professor of Russian, said Lituya. (See Sources for the full citations.)

would later translate them as meaning: "Come here," or "Follow us.") The Russians implored the natives to come closer, but the Tlingits paddled away so quickly that the slow ship could not catch them in the light airs. There were no more small boats to send in pursuit.

Two canoes later appeared momentarily. That night there was another fire on the beach.

There was nothing else to conclude but that the dark continent had swallowed the fourteen pale men. Chirikov thought that the Tlingits had either killed or captured the sailors, as did a later Soviet historian. Others believed they had drowned in the roiled waters of the entrance to either the bay or the strait.

On July 27th, nine days after the first boat disappeared, the remaining Russians departed for Kamchatka, not having set foot on shore. They were low on water and had no means of landing to refill their water casks; nor, perhaps, was there much enthusiasm for continuing what seemed like a doomed venture.

Chirikov and his crew returned safely. Bering died in a shipwreck on the homeward voyage, but the survivors feasted on sea otters and returned with the pelts, which they sold for a handsome profit, thus foreshadowing the near extinction of the species in coming years.

THE NEXT FLEETING European contact with Southeast Alaska occurred in early May of 1778.

Captain James Cook, commanding HMS *Resolution,* sailed past Lituya Bay on what was to have been his third voyage around the world. On board was a young navigator by the name of William Bligh, who was later to command the *Bounty.* (The tattered remnants of Bligh's and Lapérouse's expeditions would later cross paths in the distant South Pacific.) Captain Cook had a vague desire to rescue Chirikov's men, should they still be alive, but he sailed too far off shore to be of much help.

It was excellent weather. There were gentle breezes, and the *Resolution* and its sister ship, the *Discovery,* crawled northwestward along the coastline. Cook was concerned about a leak on the *Resolution* and flirted with the notion of seeking a protected harbor. Fortunately the leak was not serious, or his crew might have encountered the same fate as Chirikov's men.

Sailing off the coast, in the vicinity of Lituya Bay, Cook observed: "These mountains were wholly covered with Snow from the highest summit down to the Sea Coast, some few places excepted where we could perceive trees, as it were, rising their heads out of the Sea." He supposed such trunkless trees "grow on low land or islands bordering upon the Sea Coast."

Cook gave Cape Fairweather its name to counterbalance nearby Cape Foulweather. He also named Mount Fairweather, which towers above the cape—both Fairweathers being misnomers, to be sure.

In the vicinity of Yakutat Bay, a boat was put over the side with carpenters aboard to repair the leak. Cook then sailed on to his destiny. Within a year he would be hacked to death by natives on the island of Hawaii.

IT WAS THE AGE OF REASON and the late Enlightenment; and the French, being the most enlightened of all Europeans, meticulously planned what they called the "greatest of all voyages." They were looking, as others had before them, for the Northwest Passage, attempting to establish a presence on the Alaskan coast, and ascertaining the possibility of a fur trade with China. Never mind that it was near the end of the great era of exploration of the Pacific Ocean, and there was little left to discover. King Louis XVI, slow at governing but a demon at geography and other crafts related to ocean voyages, personally shaped the journey and dictated its specific objectives. The king had selected a voyage of exploration to ensure his place in history, not knowing that history had other plans for him.[†]

He chose Jean-François de Galaup, comte de Lapérouse, to command the expedition. A product of the minor nobility from the south of France, Lapérouse had joined the navy at the age of fifteen. His career alternately stagnated and took great leaps forward. The advances were aided by friends at court and acts of daring—some of substance, some not.

At a great cost of lives to the crews of his two ships, Lapérouse captured a couple of minor trading forts in Hudson Bay during the Revolutionary War and returned home a hero. The French reveled in the daring raid and individual glory, no matter the real cost. There was even a phrase, *furia francese,* that described such exploits.

Plump, socially indecisive, and ambitious, a capable commander who was skilled in the bureaucratic infighting of the *ancien régime,* Lapérouse might have remained outside the history books had it not been for the eventual disappearance of his expedition in the South Pacific.

[†]"Is there any news of Lapérouse?" the king asked on the eve of facing the guillotine in 1793. No, there was none.

The explorer had to operate under a number of royal constraints. Fainthearted Louis was adamant that there should be no deaths, whether amongst the crew from sickness and accident or to the Noble Savages from guns and swords. The king subscribed to the prevailing theories of the *philosophes,* such as Jean-Jacques Rousseau, who conjectured that native peoples lived in a state of perpetual grace.

Nothing was spared. The stores were voluminous, the personnel the best, the input of the learned societies encyclopedic, and the two hundred pages of instructions highly detailed and exceedingly daunting. That francophile Thomas Jefferson was in Paris at the time, and some twenty years later he used these preparations as a model for dispatching Lewis and Clark to the American West.

Scientists and artists, the best France had to offer, made up one component of the expedition. The commander chose mostly former shipmates to accompany him as crew members. Two of Lapérouse's relatives, less qualified than the rest, were among the officers. Napoleon Bonaparte, then a student at the Ecole Militaire, where two members of the expedition taught, expressed interest in the voyage; but another student was selected, and history continued as we know it.

The king and his designated explorer venerated Captain Cook, although England was France's traditional enemy. But Lapérouse felt compelled to distance himself from the English navigator. While in Hawaii, where he paused briefly before sailing on to Alaska, Lapérouse commented on Cook's violent death: "It is more natural for navigators to regret the loss of so great a man than coolly to examine whether some imprudence on his part might not in a manner have compelled the inhabitants of Owhyhee to have recourse to a just and necessary defense."

In his subsequent dealings with native populations, the same could have been said of Lapérouse.

THE WIND WAS FAVORABLE all the way from the Hawaiian Islands, and during the fourth week the sailors on board *L'Astrolabe* and *La Boussole* spotted the first signs of land.† Large whales surfaced around the two ships, ducks alighted on the water, and the balls and long strands of bull-whip kelp lay entwined on the surface. At four o'clock the following morning, two days after the longest day in the year of 1786, the fog lifted and a majestic chain of mountains covered with snow burst with blinding light upon the two hundred and twenty-three sailors, marines, and scientists.

The voyage, up to that point, had gone quite smoothly. There had been no illnesses or accidents during the first eleven months. But there were discomforts. The vessels, both poor sailors, were barely one hundred and thirty feet long and were crammed with provisions and equipment for a four-year journey around the world.

They had rounded treacherous Cape Horn in January weather that was reminiscent of July off the coast of France. After clearing the cape, they stopped at Concepción, Chile, relocated inland

---

†An astrolabe is an instrument for determining latitude. *Boussole* means compass. The problem of accurately fixing longitude had just been solved by the English, and the French proudly carried two of Cook's instruments.

after a tsunami spawned by an earthquake had devastated the port city. At Easter Island they viewed the "rude busts." In May they sailed past the two snow-covered volcanoes on the island of Hawaii and stopped for a day at Maui, where they observed the ravages of venereal diseases imported earlier by other European visitors.

They sailed northward and on June 23rd the glistening mountains rose precipitously in the distance. The Frenchmen should have been overjoyed to sight their destination after being at sea for so long. Instead, there was a sense of foreboding. This craggy land was not gentle France or the soft tropics. The sea broke violently against a tableland three or four hundred feet high. There was no place to land. Back from the cliff the plain was blackened, as if scourged by fire, and was totally lacking in verdure, as Lapérouse phrased it in his journal. From the bare plain rose towering walls of ice and snow.

In their first few days off this strange coast, these men of reason seem to have been confused and indecisive. They advanced and retreated gingerly, as if they sensed what lay ahead.

As they drew closer trees came into view, and it seemed as if it might be possible to find shelter among the lowlands they took to be islands. That proved to be a passing chimera. There were no islands here, just surf crashing on the broken mainland.

Suddenly, the sky darkened. Lapérouse thought it prudent to haul the wind, which set toward land, and make away until better conditions prevailed.

It cleared. They took advantage of the brief respite to make observations with their state-of-the-art instruments. They were always fixing latitude and longitude; it was one of their principal instructions. They located their physical presence with great precision in unknown waters.

The fog rolled back in, but on June 26th the weather was brilliant once again. The ships, always sailing within hailing distance of each other, coasted southeast searching for an entrance into the primeval land and a passage through it. They anchored in a dead calm at what appeared to be the mouth of a river, a channel, or a bay. The landforms were unfamiliar.

Three small boats were sent to investigate the river, the channel, or the bay. It turned out to be Yakutat Bay, but Lapérouse's men only brushed its outer fringe, where the sea broke violently on a shore littered with bleached-gray driftwood. They saw no landing place. With the barometer falling rapidly, Lapérouse made the signal to prepare to get under way; the two ships ran to the southeast to gain an offing. The wind blew hard for twenty-four hours.

On June 28th the barometer rose and the weather cleared. They took bearings on distant objects, compared results, and determined latitude and longitude. Fog shut down the coast again on June 29th, but it cleared the next day.

They stood toward the land with all sails set and spied a deep bay, most likely Dry Bay near Cape Fairweather. On closer inspection the bay turned out to be the delta of what seemed like a great river.[†] Two channels disgorged milky glacial water into the ocean.

They anchored and boats were dispatched. There was a sandbar across the river's entrance, on which the waves pounded re-

[†]The Alsek.

lentlessly. The boats shuttled back and forth for five or six hours looking for a break in the waves. There was none. A peaceful lagoon lay tantalizingly behind the line of breakers. The Frenchmen saw smoke and concluded that the land was inhabited.

They weighed anchor and again ran along the coast to the southeast, looking, always looking, for an entrance into this impenetrable land where they could take on wood and water and unpack and mount six cannons for use against the pirates expected in the China seas, whither they were bound.

At 2 P.M. the next day, after passing Mount Fairweather, they spied an inlet, behind which there appeared to be "a very fine bay." They steered toward it, and three boats were sent to probe the opening. From the sea Lapérouse viewed a long, rocky spit, which he termed a mole—a stone wall that protected a harbor. Behind the spit lay a calm bay, so wide "that nature seemed to have constructed in the remotest part of America a harbor resembling that of Toulon," Lapérouse noted, "but on a gigantic scale, adapted to her ampler powers."

The boats returned and the officers made favorable reports. They had gone in and out of the entrance several times with no difficulty, and it was deep. "Their report determined me to steer for the passage," wrote Lapérouse in his journal, which he knew was destined for the eyes of his king and the world. As they drew closer, they "perceived some savages, who made signs of friendship, by displaying and waving white mantles and different skins." [†]

[†] The quotations come from the 1807 London edition, the language of which comes closer to evoking Lapérouse's time than that of the more lit-

In the early evening the wind lessened, the tide turned, and it was impossible to make headway against the surprisingly strong ebb current. The ships were pushed out to sea, where they anchored for the night.

Lapérouse was uncertain what to do next: "The very rapid current, of which our officers had made no mention, abated my eagerness to put into this harbor." He thought it might be a trap: "I was sensible that a forced stay in a harbor, the departure from which required a combination of favorable circumstances, would be considerably detrimental to the success of my expedition."

The ships stood off and on all night.

In the morning of July 3rd Lapérouse hailed Fleuriot de Langle, the captain of *L'Astrolabe* and a long-time comrade, and they conferred. They again questioned the officers, who held firm to their favorable opinions. They had stemmed the current several times, they said. De Langle thought this was the place for their explorations to commence. "His reasons appeared to me so good, that I hesitated not to yield to them," said the commander.

Lapérouse had hitherto been following in the tracks of Cook and other explorers, but this bay was his very own discovery. He was exultant. "This port was never seen by any navigator," he exclaimed. "So that it appears to me if the French government entertained any project of establishing a trading post on this part of the coast of America, no nation could have the least pretext for opposing it." Lapérouse declared: "I give this place the name of Port des Français."

---

eral, and quite thoroughly footnoted, 1994 Hakluyt Society edition. On factual matters, I have checked the former against the latter.

But the French would only be a passing presence, and the name did not adhere. The multitude of names attached to the bay attested to the transience of its occupants and their inability to come to terms with this difficult place.[†]

At 6 A.M. the two ships, with *L'Astrolabe* in the lead, headed in a stately manner toward the entrance at what was judged to be the end of the flood current. Two small boats, acting as buoys, were stationed at each rocky point. There was a following wind. "Everything appeared to be in our favor," said Lapérouse.

The wind suddenly shifted abeam. The helmsmen threw the ships into the wind and frantically attempted to come about and retreat, but they were caught in the grip of a strong current that sucked them into the bay. Narrowly missing the rocks off Harbor Point, they anchored just inside the entrance on rocky ground.

Lapérouse was frightened: "During the thirty years that I have followed the sea I never saw two vessels so near being lost, and to have experienced such an event at the verge of the world would have enhanced our misfortunes; but we had now escaped this danger."

The tide fell rapidly, and the keels scraped the rocky bottom. The violent outgoing current tugged at the ships and threatened to drag them onto the rocks, or back through the entrance.

[†]The Tlingits called it Ltu'a, meaning "the lake within the point [or spit]." After the French departed, it was known for a time as Frenchman's Bay or Skeeter Bay, Skeeter being the phonetic equivalent of the Tlingit name for sea otter. It was also called Port Français, Skector, Entrada de Aragon, Zaliv L'tua, Altona, Alituya, Ltooa, Ltuya, Ltua, Letuya, Latuya, and Litúya bay.

The wind freshened. The sailors flew about at the various commands. Additional anchors were thrown out. The stern of *La Boussole* swung toward the rocks. Lapérouse ordered all sails struck, and the anchors finally held.

One of the officers reconnoitered the island, which seemed like an ideal spot on which to locate an observatory, and rowed a short distance beyond it. The narrow bay was choked with floating ice. Lapérouse commented: "He saw the entrance of two vast channels, but, being eager to return with an account of what he had done, had not explored them. From this report our imaginations pictured to us the possibility of penetrating into the interior of America by one of those channels."

The mythic Northwest Passage that many had sought in vain for so many years now seemed near at hand.

THE TLINGITS HAD THEIR own version of the arrival of the two French ships, as told later to Lieutenant Emmons:

> While mourning the recent drowning victims, two ships came into the bay. The people did not know what they were, but believed them to be great black birds with far reaching white wings, and, as their bird creator, Yehlh, often assumed the form of a raven, they thought that in this guise he had returned to earth, so in their fright they fled to the forest and hid. Finding after a while that no harm came to them, they crept to the shore and, gathering leaves of the skunk cabbage, they rolled them into rude telescopes and looked through them, for to see Yehlh with the naked eye was to be turned to stone.
>
> As the sails came in and the sailors climbed the rigging and ran out on the yards, in their imagination they saw the

great birds folding their wings and flocks of small black
messengers rising from their bodies and flying about. These
latter they believed to be crows, and again in fear they
sought the shelter of the woods.

One family of warriors, bolder than the rest, put on their
heavy coats of hide, the wooden collar and fighting head-
dress, and, armed with the copper knife, spear, and bow,
launched a war canoe. But scarcely had they cleared the
beach when a cloud of smoke rose from the strange appari-
tion followed by a voice of thunder, which so demoralized
them that the canoe was overturned and the occupants
scrambled to the shore as best they could.

Now one nearly blind old warrior gathered the people together, and said, that his life was far behind him and for the
common good he would see if Yehlh would turn his chil-
dren to stone, so he told his slaves to prepare his canoe, and,
putting on a robe of the sea otter, he embarked and paddled
seaward. But as he approached the ships the slaves lost heart
and would turn back, and all deserted him save two, who
finally placed him alongside.

He climbed on board, but being hardly able to distin-
guish objects, the many black forms moving about still appeared as crows, and the cooked rice that they set before
him to eat looked like worms, and he feared to touch it. He
exchanged his coat of fur for a tin pan and with presents of
food he returned to the shore.

When he landed the people crowded about surprised to
see him alive, and they touched him and smelled of him to
see if it were really he, but they could not be persuaded to
eat the strange food that he had brought to them.

After much thought the old man was convinced that it
was not Yehlh that he had gone to and that the black figures

must be people, so the natives, profiting by his experience, visited the ships and exchanged their furs for many strange articles.

It was at this time that two boats were lost at the mouth of the bay and many of the white men were drowned.

AT FIRST THINGS WENT WELL. The Tlingits received the Europeans with the ceremony that demonstrated they were ready to trade. Ceremonies were a large part of the Tlingits' culture, just as they were for the French.

An invocation and singing, followed by dancing—all with the proper responses—preceded formal trading with equals. With social inferiors, weaker people, or those who did not respond in the proper manner, the Tlingits merely seized what they coveted.

A large canoe, the type that was used in warfare, slipped out from the encampment near the entrance and made toward *Boussole*. The canoe was hewed from red cedar and held twenty-one men. The high prow and the curved stern were undercut like a gondola's; but the graceful canoe was vastly more seaworthy than the Venetian craft, thought the Europeans.

Such an elegant vessel, some forty-five feet in length—that being roughly one-third the length of *La Boussole*—belonged to a house chief. The paddlers dipped their oars in unison, and the vessel shot forward. As the canoe cleaved the water, a tall figure stood in the stern and gradually raised his arms to the sky. "Before he came on board, he appeared to address a prayer to the sun. He then made a long harangue, which was concluded by a kind of song, by no means disagreeable, and greatly resembling the chant of our churches," Lapérouse observed.

The canoe circled the ship, and the chief could be seen more clearly. He was a bearded man, with long hair that cascaded down his back. His nose was pierced by a copper ornament, and he wore a conical helmet atop his head. His leathery skin hung in folds. He looked disgusting to the French officers and sailors, who crossed and recrossed the deck in order to keep the circling craft in sight.

To the Tlingits, the strangers appeared to gibber away like angry crows.

The canoe eventually came alongside. The chief and his entourage climbed up a rope ladder to the deck of the ship, and the representatives of the two races appraised one another. Lapérouse had instructed his crew to display respect.

The Tlingits waited, but there was no response. So with waning conviction, they launched into the last part of the ceremony that initiated trade between equals. For nearly an hour they danced in grave steps that matched the rhythm of their voices. Lapérouse then distributed small gifts and dismissed them, giving the Tlingits no chance to reciprocate.

THE WELCOMING PARTY DEPARTED, and the French moved their ships to a safer anchorage on the far side of the island.

A lively trade soon commenced. Lapérouse was astonished by the trading skills of the Indians, whom he compared with "the ablest buyers in Europe." Trading was sport, entertainment, and survival for the Tlingits.

Indians in canoes clustered around the two ships. The French sought otter skins. The Tlingits traded for hatchets, adzes, and bar iron. Skins to generate wealth; iron to aid warfare. The items flew back and forth with great avidity between the two races.

Lapérouse foresaw the start of a great trading enterprise in sea otter furs. Missing the playful qualities and anthropomorphic characteristics of the otters, he went to the heart of the matter for the French: "The sea otter is an amphibious animal, better known for the beauty of its skin than by any accurate description."

The two frigates—their three masts and numerous spars being but puny matchsticks set against the massive mountains—swung slowly back and forth on their anchors. Their squat bulks were at the mercy of the sharp winds that swept down off the mountains or roared in from the gulf and the strong tidal currents that rushed past the island.

The French erected an observatory on the north side of the island and set about determining their exact position. Sailmakers, coopers, and the smith were sent ashore, and tents were erected on the beach for these craftsmen, who set about repairing the torn sails and water casks that had begun to leak. Much to the disgust of the Tlingits, the island soon became a bustling French colony.

Lapérouse thought they would be secure from theft on the island, but the Tlingits were soon pilfering from the French. The island was as easily accessible to them as it was to the occasional grizzly bear that swam across the channels on either side.

As was his wont, Lapérouse underestimated his native adversaries: "Experience had taught us that the Indians are great thieves; but we did not suspect them of sufficient activity and perseverance to carry into execution difficult and tedious schemes. In a short time we learned to know them better."

The French had proved themselves inferiors and had infringed upon the Tlingits' territory and their rights to natural resources—such as fresh water, firewood, and fish—without just compensation. The Indians retaliated. They set about taking everything in sight.

Ever mindful of the instructions of their king, the French attempted to gently dissuade the Tlingits from stealing, a crime that was extremely offensive to the Europeans and was punishable by imprisonment in their own country. Lapérouse established the Spartan law amongst his men, meaning that the person robbed was punished.

He called a group of Tlingits together and had a marine fire his musket into a sample of their wooden armor that he had purchased. The ball pierced the vest. He fired off a cannon to demonstrate that objects could be destroyed from a distance. Next, an expert marksmen shot birds from the sky. These demonstrations of armed might were for naught.

A few nights after the observatory was established on the island, a small band of Tlingits landed on the opposite shore and, in the words of Lapérouse, "creeping on their bellies like snakes, almost without stirring a leaf," crossed the island through the thick woods the French had been unable to penetrate during the day.

A dozen marines were on guard duty around the small encampment. The Tlingits glided past the perimeter guards and into the very tent of the observatory, where two officers slept. They then crawled back past the guards, carrying with them a silver-mounted musket and the officers' clothes that had been carefully folded beneath their pillows, the better to preserve the creases. But the greatest loss, when the burglary was discovered the next morning, was the sheet of paper on which all the astronomical observations had been made since their arrival in Port des Français.

THE FRENCH MOVED off the island and hastened their preparations for departure. Shore parties under the command of armed officers took on wood and water. The summer season was fast approaching, and Lapérouse wanted to visit Monterey in Alta California before the onslaught of winter storms and their departure for Asia.

But first they needed to explore the headwaters of the bay in order to ascertain whether "we might penetrate into the interior of America." Lapérouse added, "We conjectured it might lead to some large river, taking its course between two of the mountains, and originating from one of the great lakes north of Canada." One of those "lakes" was Hudson Bay, with which Lapérouse was personally familiar.

Lapérouse and de Langle provisioned two boats and set off with a retinue of officers, scientists, and artists. The two crews rowed across the smooth water toward the head of the bay, which Lapérouse described as "perhaps the most extraordinary place in the world." He added, "To form an idea of it, it is necessary to conceive a basin of water, unfathomable in the middle, bordered by peaked mountains, of great height, covered with snow, and without one blade of grass to decorate this vast heap of rocks, condemned by nature to eternal sterility."

The calm was so great that the voice of a man or the cry of a gull could be heard from a great distance, as could the crack and splash of huge chunks of glacial ice falling into the bay.

They turned left into what they labeled a cul de sac on their detailed map of the port. The enormous glacier that spilled into Gilbert Inlet from the mountains and ended in precipitous cliffs that towered above the small boats dashed any hopes of an easy entrance into the interior of America. Some officers boldly mounted Lituya Glacier, at great risk to themselves, "but they could only perceive one continued mass of ice and snow," said Lapérouse.

It was a miracle no Frenchmen were killed that day. A large block of glacial ice fell into the deep bay. A wave swept across the water, lifted one of the boats, and deposited it upon the land. Fortunately, Lapérouse had been standing some distance above the water. The boat was repaired and returned to its proper element.

The disappointed explorers rowed back to the vessels, "having finished our voyage into the interior of America in a few hours," commented Lapérouse rather dryly.

Never a true believer in the existence of a Northwest Passage, but certainly not one to ignore the instructions of his king, Lapérouse also employed irony to describe the purchase of the island.

The next day an imposing Tlingit—whom Lapérouse identified as *the* chief, although he knew no such single authority existed—accompanied by a large escort came on board *La Boussole* and offered, at least that was the convenient interpretation, to sell the island to the French. "Tacitly reserving, no doubt," Lapérouse said, "to himself and the other Indians, the right of robbing us upon it." Crossed out in the original journal was the added phrase: "as much as they could."

Although doubting the chief's right to conclude such a negotiation on behalf of the diverse population, but allowing himself to be persuaded by the presence of so many Tlingits, who surely, he reasoned, must represent a consensus, Lapérouse concluded the deal for what would become known as Cenotaph Island with some red cloth, axes, adzes, iron bars, and nails.

He thereupon took possession of the small island in the name of the king of France. A bottle with a note recording the transaction in official language was buried, as were bronze medals that had been struck before they left France. Except for some furs, later sold at very low prices, the island was their only tangible, albeit brief, acquisition in the Northwest.

The chart of the bay was completed, and wood and water were replenished. There was nothing left to do but take soundings at the entrance and then quit this forlorn land. Lapérouse emphasized what had already been made clear in order to soften what came next: "In short, we considered ourselves as the most fortunate of navigators, in having arrived at such a distance from Europe without having had a single person sick, and without an individual of either crew being attacked with the scurvy."

BUT ALAS, Lapérouse lamented, "Here the greatest of misfortunes, and most impossible to be foreseen, awaited us." Following the tragic events of July 13th, a lachrymose Lapérouse retreated to his ornate cabin and penned the following passage:

> It is with the most pungent sorrow that I proceed to give the history of a disaster a thousand times more cruel than disease, and all the other events incident to long voyages. But I submit to the severe duty I have imposed upon myself of writing this account; and I am not ashamed to avow, that my sorrow for the event has a hundred times since moistened my cheeks with tears; that time has not effaced my grief; and that every object, every moment, recalls to my remembrance our loss, at a time when we had so little reason to apprehend such a disaster.

The day began in a pleasant enough manner. Lapérouse organized a bird hunt and breakfast outing for his officers with the additional purpose of taking soundings at the entrance to the bay.

It was a brilliantly clear morning, one of those rare, tranquil days that delude the casual visitor into believing that all is peaceful. The French sailors were in good spirits. Soon they would leave this bleak landscape and set sail for sunny California, the domain of the relatively civilized Spaniards.

The three officers who were in command of the three small boats were the cream of their country's aristocracy and navy. They had medals, campaigns, and backgrounds in common.

Charles-Gabriel Morel d'Escures, a commander of warships, second officer of *La Boussole,* thirty-five years old and impulsive, commanded that ship's pinnace and the expedition of pleasure and mild work. In his boat went Pierre de Montarnal, a *garde de la marine* and a distant relative of the childless Lapérouse, who regarded him as a son.

Lieutenant Charles Boutin had charge of *La Boussole*'s jolly boat. The son of a powerful *intendant des finances,* the stolid Boutin had taken part in the capture of Grenada and the battle of Savannah, been captured by the English, commanded two ships of war, and received the Cross of Saint Louis.

Edouard de Laborde de Marchainville, an ensign in his mid-twenties, commanded *L'Astrolabe*'s pinnace. A gentle man well versed in naval sciences, he was the scion of a financial dynasty with close ties to the king. With him on this fateful day went his younger brother, Midshipman Boutervillers. It was the first time that de Langle had permitted the two brothers to go together in the same party. Their fervent pleas that they be allowed to shoot and have breakfast together under the trees won his consent.

Lapérouse was quite mindful of d'Escures's zest for adventure. The night before the outing he called the lieutenant to his cabin and handed him written orders for the next day. He then related why he had formalized the order.

Much offended, d'Escures cut his commander short.

"Do you take me for a child? I have commanded ships of war!"

Holding up his hand, Lapérouse calmly explained that he and de Langle had sounded the passage two days before, and that the officer in charge of the other pinnace had passed so close to the point that the boat's bottom scraped the rocks.

"I know young officers think it a feather in their caps to mount the parapets of the trenches during a siege; and the same spirit leads them to brave rocks and breakers in boats," Lapérouse continued. "But please consider, my dear sir, such inconsiderate boldness might be attended with the most fatal consequences in such an expedition as ours."

He read the lengthy orders out loud, first to d'Escures and then to Boutin, who had been summoned to the cabin as a witness. Lapérouse was careful to copy the detailed instructions in his journal.

D'Escures was "expressly ordered" not to approach the passage if there were any breakers. The best time to pass through the entrance was at 8:30 A.M., he was advised, when the water was slack. Lapérouse scribbled in the margin of his journal: "and at 7:15 he was drowned."

"After instructions like these, could I entertain any apprehensions?" Lapérouse queried his king and posterity.

The island blocked the view of the entrance, so it was not until the three boats emerged from behind it early that morning that the three officers could perceive the line of breakers that sealed the passage.

The boats left perfect wakes in the placid water, which mirrored the white peaks and the dark forest. The still water was deceptive. Unbeknownst to the excursionists, the powerful current was speeding out of Lituya Bay.

D'Escures's pinnace was in the lead, Boutin's jolly boat was next, and Marchainville's pinnace brought up the rear. D'Escures set a fast pace. When Boutin approached, d'Escures pulled ahead. Much to the annoyance of Boutin, d'Escures repeated this childish maneuver every time the other boat neared.

The sailors and marines rowed while the chief pilot heaved the lead and called off the marks, which were duly recorded on the chart.

At 7:15 the lead pinnace halted about a thousand feet from the entrance, allowing the jolly boat to catch up at last. Marchainville's pinnace was three-quarters of a mile distant.

Ascertaining that the breakers were impenetrable, d'Escures made his decision. He called to Boutin, "I believe we can do nothing better than go to breakfast, for the sea breaks terribly in the passage."

Boutin replied, "I think so too; and I fancy we must content ourselves with fixing the limits of the sandy-bottomed bay on the larboard of the entrance."

Another officer was about to shout something to Boutin from d'Escures's boat, when he happened to glance at the land. Boutin quickly followed his gaze. The land was flying past. The distance to the pounding breakers, which could now be heard more distinctly, had been halved since they had stopped but a few moments ago.

Their concern, however, was not great. They thought that they could easily stem the current and row to shore. But to no avail. They were held in an implacable grip that sucked them into the narrow passage.

The two boats plunged from smooth water into a froth of broken waves. The oarsmen were splashed by dollops of water as they continued to pull in unison toward shore. Spent waves broke over the gunwales. The growing roar of fresh breakers obliterated shouted commands. Discipline began to give way to confusion.

Boutin threw an anchor overboard, but it did not hold. Unattached to any stanchion, the anchor and line slid overboard.

The two boats were tossed about; the oarsmen were thrown from side to side. They could not get a firm bite on the water, and their rhythm disintegrated. From a disciplined military unit, they collapsed into a band of badly frightened men.

Faces swiveled about. Masks of obedience gave way to oaths and screams of terror. Mouths opened, but sounds could not be heard within the howling maelstrom.

The sailors gripped the gunwales. An oar was lost. Two, four, five more oars were swept away. The pinnace slithered sideways to the breakers. D'Escures raised his arms, as if imploring God. Cold, numbing water poured into the boat.

Boutin's crew quickly found themselves in the midst of the largest waves, which almost filled their boat, yet it still answered the helm. Boutin was able to hold the stern toward the breakers, and this gave him hope.[†] While poised atop a wave, he saw the

---

[†] Nowadays this maneuver is well known to boatmen who row through whitewater rapids.

other boat sixty to eighty yards away, half submerged and minus its crew and oars.

Boutin looked about and saw that the waves formed an un-broken chain across the entrance. If they could row a hundred yards to the east, there was a slight chance of weathering a less-dangerous sea.

Between the solid sheets of ice-cold water that inundated them, the rowers pulled with desperation toward shore. By 7:25 — ten minutes after d'Escures's decision to make for shore—they were out of danger. The shivering sailors bailed their boat, then looked about.

All seemed hopeless. No swimmer could possibly overcome the current or survive the violent agitation of the frigid water for more than a few moments.

Nevertheless, they went in search of their comrades. They rowed with great trepidation in the quieter water. Every few moments they saw an object float by and feared it might be a body. It proved to be either a seal, an otter, or drifting seaweed.

When the jolly boat was lifted high atop a large swell, even when Boutin was hoisted upon the shoulders of a fellow officer, they could still see no sign of the other boats or the sailors who had been in such high spirits just a few moments earlier.

They passed through the remainder of the entrance on calmer swells. Boutin spotted figures on shore waving what appeared to be cloaks. He thought it was Marchainville and his crew, who were waiting for slack water to come to their rescue.

At 8:45 there were no breakers across the passage, just a heavy swell. Boutin searched in the direction the ebb current would have carried d'Escures and his men, but saw nothing.

At 9 o'clock the flood current set in and, with a depleted crew to consider and the possibility that they might not be able to enter the passage on the full force of the flood, Boutin headed back into the bay on smooth water.

He kept toward the spit. When he drew near, he saw that it had not been Frenchmen who had waved, but rather Tlingits wearing fur capes. The natives made signs that two boats had sunk in the entrance.

A saddened Boutin hoped that he had misunderstood, or that the Tlingits had lied to him. When he reached the ships on the other side of the island at 10 o'clock and was told that Marchainville had not returned, he concluded that his brave shipmates had attempted to save their comrades and perished.

"Assuredly a glorious death," concluded the lieutenant.

Upon reflection, Boutin was puzzled by the great force of the current that had so quickly and silently grasped the three boats. It had been d'Escures's plan just to approach the entrance, he insisted to Lapérouse. Where they had paused should have been distance enough to ensure their safety.

To see the land flying by with such "extreme velocity" had greatly astonished him. Why, just two days before, neither Lapérouse nor de Langle had had any problem going out with the ebb and returning with the flood. There must have been "special circumstances" on the 13th of July, he concluded.

Soon after Boutin's return, de Langle came on board *La Boussole* to confer with Lapérouse. De Langle related that the two brothers had been in one of the lost boats. Lapérouse said his relative was among the missing. Tears coursed down the cheeks of the two comrades.

Lapérouse then lashed out at d'Escures's poor judgment and at the voracious savages who surrounded the two ships at that very moment and, like a Greek chorus, were chanting news of the drownings and presence of the new Land Otter Men.

Although he would have preferred to reply with a broadside, Lapérouse answered in the only way he could, considering the king's wishes. He showered the Indians with gifts and raked them with his pen. "Nothing could be more powerful in awakening their humanity [than gifts]," he noted. "They now hasten to the shore and spread themselves over both sides of the bay [to look for bodies]."

Lapérouse dispatched boats to search for survivors; none were found on the black sand beaches. Twenty-one men had been drowned within moments, balanced against not a single life lost in eleven months. His mood veered toward the dark side; bitterness and depression replaced self-assuredness.

"NOTHING REMAINED FOR US but to quit with speed a country that had proved so fatal," wrote Lapérouse. But there were appearances to consider; he owed the families of the missing men a few days' search. His countrymen would not understand "that the fury of the waves in that place left no hope of their return."

The expedition lingered. The weather turned against the French, and a few days stretched into seventeen before they could depart that cursed place.

The furies were unleashed. Strong gales raked the bay from the gulf, and fierce winds tore down from the high peaks swathed in thick clouds. The ships were tossed about and barely held their ground.

The French constructed a monument of stones upon the newly named island. Underneath the cairn they buried a bottle with an account of the tragedy. It was five days before they could move from behind Cenotaph Island to an anchorage nearer the Tlingit settlement in the northwest corner of the bay.

Should any of the twenty-one men have survived, the thinking went, their comrades could more easily spot them from this vantage point near the entrance. Then contrary winds sealed the ships in the bay for another twelve days.

They waited. For hours on end they watched the entrance of the bay through a telescope. Lapérouse noted the great respect the Tlingits displayed for the entrance to the bay.

On July 22nd there was news. A canoe pulled alongside *La Boussole,* and four Indians handed up some pieces of wreckage from the boats and made signs that they had recovered a body. Lapérouse dispatched a search party consisting of three officers.

The Tlingits were inundated with cheap gifts. They promised to lead the officers to the body, or this was what the French believed them to say. Considering the Indians' great fear of Land Otter Men, it was doubtful whether they wanted to get anywhere near such an object.

There was a rough trail south along the coast that alternately bisected the thick forest and black sand and boulder-strewn beach. The round boulders were particularly difficult to walk across because they were slippery. The officers lagged behind, and soon the bare-foot natives had outdistanced them.

They called. The Tlingits reappeared, were given more trinkets, and disappeared again—this time for good. The officers returned and made their report. Lapérouse wrote: "We were not surprised at the account they gave us of the stratagems of the savages, who in knavery and theft were unparalleled."

WITH TIME ON THEIR HANDS, the French explored the bay and its immediate surroundings more fully. They managed to desecrate two Tlingit burial grounds in the process of gaining insight into native customs.

They termed a burial ground near the village on the south shore of the bay a *morai,* giving it the Polynesian designation. One of the artists sketched the scene. The more agile sailors and scientists hoisted themselves atop a wooden platform supported by four posts.

They opened a box. Inside they found cremated ashes and a mummified head, most likely that of a shaman. The head was tightly wrapped in skins. They unwound the skins, thus exposing the head to the deleterious effect of the moist air. After carefully examining the head and taking measurements, they replaced it "with scrupulous exactness, adding presents of iron and beads."

The Tlingits were uneasy, an understatement since witches were known to scatter similar small items about the dead, thus endangering the living. The trinkets were placed on two successive days and were twice removed, demonstrating the Tlingits' supposed greed to the French.

At another burial site the explorers found more cremated remains and the surviving canoe from the recent disaster at the mouth of the bay. They surmised that the natives had most likely come from elsewhere, since the sealskin-framed canoe did not resemble local craft. They measured the covering, sewn with the exactitude of European workmanship, and briefly considered taking it back to France. It was left out of respect for the dead.

The living, as well as the dead, were ravished. The French repeatedly descended upon the villages, and the Tlingit men rushed to hide their wives, described by Lapérouse as "the most disgusting beings in the world." Those crew members "not of the most delicate taste" copulated with the women in the open after they "were overcome with presents," thus sowing the diseases that would decimate the Tlingits in coming years.

While Lapérouse had little use for the natives, to the point where his French editor felt it necessary to excuse him on the grounds of his recent loss, he thought the place idyllic. There was no better location to establish a trading post and fort, he noted. Nowhere else in the Pacific Northwest could furs be gathered in such great quantities. A single battery of four guns could command the entrance and put any invasion force to route. The fort, magazines, warehouses, and lodgings could be constructed on Cenotaph Island, which had sufficient wood, water, and soil to cultivate.

The surrounding land was a virtual cornucopia. Wild celery, sorrel, lupine, wild peas, yarrow, succory, and bastard foxglove were gathered and put in soups, ragouts, and salads. The lowlands near the bay were filled with raspberries, strawberries, and gooseberries. The rivers abounded with trout and salmon, while one-hundred-pound halibut were caught in the bay. Mussels lay in heaps upon the intertidal rocks. There were plentiful amounts of game in the forests.

Lapérouse had the good fortune to visit the bay at the height of its seasonal fecundity. An account of winter was lacking.

Also missing was a description of a recent natural phenomenon of gigantic proportions, but how were these Europeans to know of such things as the rapid movement of sea-level glaciers or giant waves? Although the evidence was writ large upon the bay, it would take scientists another one hundred and seventy-five years to decode it.

Two sketches by the landscape artist who accompanied the expedition, Duché de Vancy, show a neatly shaved tree line along the lower reaches of the hills surrounding the bay. The exactitude of the cut on the north side, which matches the steady grade of the lateral moraine known as Solomon Railroad, strongly suggests a very recent, rapid retreat of the glacier that filled the fjord.

There is another possible explanation. Since geologists estimate that the last glacier to scour the bay retreated two hundred years before Lapérouse's visit, conceivably the bare rock and dirt depicted in the drawing indicate the very recent passage of a giant wave.

THE WEATHER TOOK a turn for the better, and the French departed with haste. *L'Astrolabe* and *La Boussole* weighed anchor on July 30th and, aided by a favorable breeze and current, cleared the entrance with no difficulty.

Lituya Bay would not immediately release the two ships, however. The winds were light and varied, and fog enveloped the vessels day and night. They hovered just offshore.

They sailed upon a ghost-like sea, and land was but a fleeting mirage.

Lapérouse named a cape in honor of Chirikov, the Russian navigator whose men had disappeared.

On August 8th they finally lost sight of Mount Crillon, which towers above Lituya Bay.[†]

SAILING SOUTHWARD they could see a mountain, perhaps Mount Shasta in northern California, in full volcanic eruption. After passing by the mouth of Tomales Bay and Point Reyes in dense fog, the two ships anchored off the Spanish settlement of Monterey in mid-September. They were the first foreign vessels to visit Alta California and left an invaluable record of the region's natural surroundings and the Spanish colony's human institutions.

From Monterey Lapérouse wrote his minister a carefully worded letter to accompany the portion of his journal that recounted the events in Lituya Bay. "I make bold to claim that no other plan of voyage has been so vast," he began. "You will be happy to tell the King, My Lord, that so far not one drop of Indian blood has been shed, nor is there a sick man in the *Boussole.*"

Then, backing into the matter, he described the tragedy. Lapérouse recounted the loss of his beloved relative and two distinguished officers, adding, "as for M. d'Escures, his foolishness and his pretentious vanity, pitting himself against rocks and currents that are beyond all human efforts, were the cause of our misfortunes."

They left California and sailed on and on across a trackless ocean. Three months later they made a perfect landfall at Macao,

[†]Mount Crillon was named for Lapérouse's friend the comte de Crillon, a general. Crillon's home on the Place de la Concorde in Paris would become the luxurious Hôtel de Crillon. Subsequently, a glacier, lake, river, and inlet in the Lituya Bay region would receive the same name.

where they were briefly reunited with their naval counterparts and obtained news of home. The anticipated arrival of English ships bearing furs from the Northwest had depressed the market, so what they had obtained in Lituya Bay was sold for a pittance. The best furs were sent to Queen Marie Antoinette.

Sailing from Macao to Manila, then northward along the coast of Asia, the French believed they were the first Europeans to explore the East China Sea and the Sea of Japan.

From the Kamchatka Peninsula, whence Bering and Chirikov had set sail, Lapérouse dispatched his young Russian interpreter to the court of Louis XVI with correspondence and his journals. Jean-Baptiste Barthélemy de Lesseps's travels across the Siberian wilderness rated its own published journal. De Lesseps, uncle of Ferdinand de Lesseps, the builder of the Suez Canal and the first to attempt to construct a sea-level canal across the Panamanian isthmus, would become one of the fortunate few who departed the voyage in time to survive it.

Turning south to Australia, the French hurried to beat the first English colonists to New South Wales. They anchored off the Samoan island of Tutuila in December of 1787. The voyage had been extremely taxing; their tropical desires were heightened; their guard was down.

There were incidents with the stoutly built natives, and finally a pitched battle erupted in what became known as Massacre Bay. Twelve Frenchmen were killed; twenty were severely wounded. There was no estimate of the number of Samoans killed and wounded. De Langle, Lapérouse's constant shadow in *L'Astrolabe,* was among the fallen, and his bitter commander squarely placed the blame for the tragedy upon his dead comrade.

They reached Botany Bay eighteen years after Cook's first visit and six days after the arrival of an English fleet bearing a human cargo of seven hundred convicts. The English soon moved, finding a better harbor at what would become known as Sydney. The French fended off native depredations in Botany Bay and apologetically returned escaped convicts to their nearby captors.

A robust Lapérouse had left France at the age of forty-three. Now, nearly three years later, he had lost all his hair and teeth and muttered about "secret presentiments." *L'Astrolabe* and *La Boussole* departed on March 10th, 1788, from Australia and headed toward Tonga.

The two vessels and their crews were never seen again by European eyes.

FRANCE BECAME EMBROILED in the madness of revolution. But that did not prevent the equivalent of a modern media frenzy evolving around the tragic disappearance of a national hero. Lapérouse was most often depicted as having been shipwrecked in a tropical paradise, where he was surrounded by comely native women who ministered to all his earthly desires. The reality, of course, was quite different.[†]

[†]The Lapérouse legend was later recounted in Jules Verne's *Twenty Thousand Leagues under the Sea*. Captain Nemo opens the panels in the salon of the submarine *Nautilus* and shows the professor Lapérouse's final resting place on a coral reef. Fish swim through the wreck of a vessel carpeted with living flowers. "'Ah! it is a fine death for a sailor!' Captain Nemo says. 'A coral tomb makes a quiet grave; and I trust that I and my comrades will find no other.'"

In 1791, Captain Edward Edwards of the British navy sailed past an uncharted isle that would become known as Vanikoro Island. Here the two ill-fated expeditions, one English and the other French, nearly touched.

Edwards was searching for Fletcher Christian and the remainder of the *Bounty* mutineers, having already captured fourteen on Tahiti. He saw "very thick smoke" rising from the island but did not pause in his relentless search that also ended in shipwreck. Captain Edwards was later called a "blinkered horse" for missing this obvious signal.

Two years later the two rescue vessels that had been dispatched from France, having been delayed by revolution and timidity, slipped past the same island in the Santa Cruz group. The captains of both ships and half their crews died of various illnesses. The vessels were seized by the Dutch, who were at war with the French.

Finally, it was a rogue Irish sea captain financed by British mercantile interests who located the remains of the French expedition on the reef off Vanikoro in 1827.[†] Peter Dillon arrived on the island shortly after the last French survivor had died, those preceding him having fallen victim to shipwreck, battles with the natives, and sickness.

A French vessel, hastily renamed *L'Astrolabe,* set sail to confirm the finding. Half the crew was stricken with a mysterious fever on the island, most probably malaria. With a sick captain

---

[†]The Vanikoro reef on which the two ships were wrecked achieved a measure of scientific fame. It is described in Charles Darwin's monograph *The Structure and Distribution of Coral Reefs* (1842).

in command, the skeleton crew barely managed to extricate itself from the island that had claimed Lapérouse's expedition.

Captain Dumont d'Urville, who later discovered the famed statue of Venus de Milo, wrote of their escape: "And so, despite our exhausted condition, after several anxious minutes when we saw that we had cleared the reefs of this ill-fated island, all of us experienced a surge of joy similar to that felt by a prisoner who has escaped the horrors of the most inhuman captivity."

CHAPTER V.

THE RUSSIANS.

_____

LIKE MUCH OF THE HISTORY of other frontier lands, and the American West in particular, the pattern in Southeast Alaska was to probe tentatively, exploit commercially, explore scientifically, and then settle. For the remainder of the century the Spanish, French, English, Americans, and Russians probed the coast and one another's intentions.

In the waning years of the 1780s, some thirty foreign vessels hovered at times off the coast of Alaska. Their purpose was, according to a Russian report, "to attempt to cultivate the acquaintance of the tribes allied with us and, in the long run, to make them tributary to their country."

Two years after the departure of the French, the Russian galliot *Three Saints* entered Lituya Bay and anchored off Cenotaph Island. The mission of the Russians was to secretly bury any evidence of prior possession and thus preempt the claims of other European nations.

The Russians found many tools, implements, and an anchor—all embossed with the royal *fleur de lis.* The Tlingits told them that foreign vessels had visited two years previously. There is no mention by the Russians in their accounts of the mound of stones, the two buried bottles, and the bronze medals on Cenotaph Island, which either the Tlingits or the Russians themselves may have removed.

The Russians left their marks in other parts of the bay: a buried copper (or iron) plate bearing an inscription stating "Russian Territory" and a wooden cross. They claimed the bay for Catherine the Great and accepted what they conveniently interpreted to be an offering of fealty from the chief, whom they suitably reimbursed.

A lively trade in furs and iron ensued. One stormy night the Tlingits stole an anchor belonging to the Russians, who did not linger, noting "the dangers of this place." They departed without incident at "full tide."

A memorandum describing "Ltua Bay" was forwarded to Catherine in 1790. It stated:

> It is inhabited by the Koloshes [Tlingits] who have been brought under Russian domination. One emblem and one board, number 19, were left there. The toyon [chief], as a token of his loyalty, made a gift of one sea-otter. All these islands and bays, as well as those not enumerated here but mentioned in the first memorandum, abound in timber and other resources. As for the inhabitants, they have already become more attached to the Russian traders than to the foreigners who used to visit them.

A more fulsome report by the governor-general of the easternmost Russian province, who oversaw Alaskan affairs, elaborated on the advantages of Yakutat and Lituya bays. The empress was told:

> The first bay, called Yakutat Bay and the second, called Litua Bay, are endowed by nature itself not only with favorable location but with abundance in everything. Both of them are distinguished by the vastness of their areas and the

number of their inhabitants. . . . In spite of everything, even of opposition to their savagery, they [the resident Tlingits] all with one mind, as a result of the affable attitude toward them on the part of the Company, came not only to understand the grandeur of Your Empire but to give themselves up into complete obedience to it.

The fur trade flourished, for a time. The Russians explored one bay after another, and their Aleut hunters followed with an armed escort and speared, clubbed, and shot the sea otters. The waters of Southeast Alaska ran red. Lituya Bay was not spared; nor, in return, did it spare.

A strange character—an Englishman, seemingly a mercenary, and perhaps a spy—made a brief appearance on the scene. His name varies, and he is an elusive presence in the archives, surfacing here and there, as does the history of Alaska and Lituya Bay during this interregnum. The sources are not wholly reliable and are sometimes contradictory, but they can be forged into a story, and that is what counts.

Although a navigator and shipbuilder by profession, James George Shields served in the Russian military service for a time.[†] He then returned to the sea as a sublieutenant for the Russian mercantile interests, who were seeking to develop the Alaskan fur trade.

Shields oversaw the construction of the packet-boat *Northern Eagle* in Okhotsk on the Kamchatka Peninsula. He then sailed the vessel to Kodiak, where Alexander Baranov was in charge of

---

[†]The Russian-American Company's historian, P. A. Tikhmenev, gives Shields's russified name as Iakov Egorovich Shil'ts.

the company's interests. On board were all the manufactured items needed to build a ship. The Russian colonists were henceforth expected to be self-reliant in shipbuilding. Shields helped with construction of the first ship built in the colony, the three-masted, seventy-three-foot *Phoenix.*

Baranov did not trust the foreigner. The instructions from his home office said not to alienate Shields, but to ply him with "promises of rewards," so that he did not "seek his fortune elsewhere." It was good advice, for Shields had vainly sought to make contact with the English explorer George Vancouver, who was sailing along the gulf coast at this time.

Shields was dispatched eastward in the *Northern Eagle.* The historian Hubert Howe Bancroft wrote, "Rumors of the existence of unknown islands, rich in seals and sea-otters, in various parts of the new possession had been afloat for some time." The Englishman was sent to find these riches. Shields was also to ask any Indians that he encountered along the way if they, or neighboring tribes, held any Europeans as slaves. "It was thought that some of La Pérouse's men might have escaped drowning, only to fall into the hands of the savage inhabitants of the country," Bancroft explained.

With Aleut slaves manning a fleet of four hundred and fifty bidarkas that accompanied the heavily armed *Northern Eagle,* Shields entered Lituya Bay in July of 1796, almost to the day a decade after Lapérouse's visit. The mother ship and its accompanying swarm must have seemed like an invading army to the Tlingits. The resulting carnage was commensurate with the large numbers of hunters. Nearly two thousand sea otters were killed in a few days.

Shields described Lituya Bay in a report to Baranov:

The entrance is most dangerous; the strong currents, rushing over hidden rocks occasion rapids which almost entirely conceal the channel, and thus add to the danger. In fair weather my vessel was being [pulled] in, when the water [behind] me appeared one and a half fathoms higher than in the bay, and we shot the descent with irresistible speed and great danger.[†]

Once inside, all immediate danger ceased. The bay is large and filled with rocks and sands; no wood at the immediate entrance, and no position for a settlement. The bay is destitute of fish, except halibut, which abound only in spring and summer. In the winter the bay abounds in sea lions, but the common seal is seldom seen.

Three years later Shields was in command of the *Phoenix,* bound from the Russian mainland to the struggling colony. The following account was written by William H. Dall of the Smithsonian Institution, an early explorer of Alaska: "The Company's vessel *Fenie* [Phoenix] with its newly consecrated bishop Joásaph, eighty-eight passengers, and a valuable cargo, in charge of Captain Shultz, was lost with all on board. Most of the ecclesiastics were on this vessel, and it is said that from this time to 1810 only one monk was left in the colonies."[‡]

[†]One and one-half fathoms would be nine feet, a considerable drop.

[‡]Shields, Shil'ts, Shiltz (Davidson, 1869), and Shultz; they all seem to be the same person. P. A. Tikhmenev wrote: "It was suspected that the loss of the ship was caused by the terrible fever then raging in Okhotsk and Kamchatka. If the crew succumbed to this infection, owing to the poor and crowded conditions on board, they may have been unable to bring the ship to its destination."

The northern Gulf of Alaska was awash with wreckage in 1799. The *Northern Eagle* was also lost, with twenty-two thousand otter skins on board. Many Russian vessels sank or were wrecked because of inexperienced captains and crews, faulty construction, and stormy seas.

The Russians returned to Lituya Bay that same year to hunt sea otter again. This time there was no mother ship; rather, two or three Russians accompanied the Aleut hunters in their frail bidarkas across the stormy gulf, where they faced "the anger of the Tlingits who bitterly resented this poaching on their hunting grounds," according to the ethnologist Frederica de Laguna, who carefully examined nineteenth-century documents as they related to the Tlingits.

Near the end of the century there was a decided shift in power. The Tlingits began acquiring guns from New England merchant vessels in exchange for furs. De Laguna wrote: "I think it more likely that these firearms had been obtained from American traders, not from the Spanish, British, or Russians, since the reckless 'Boston Men' had apparently neither scruples nor fear of arming the Tlingits, provided they made their own quick profits."

The English, however, also armed the Tlingits. Both countries and their mercantile interests had much to gain from weakening the Russian hold on Alaska. And it is very possible that merchants from the countries involved in the trade of arms cheated the Tlingits. Lieutenant Emmons noted: "It is on record that trading vessels sold the natives muskets with the lock-spring partly sawed through, which shortly broke and rendered the guns useless. Upon the return trip of the vessel, these were repurchased for a trifle, and after being repaired and again tampered with, were resold to the Indians."

The Tlingits used the weapons that fired correctly with devastating effect. They destroyed the Russian-American Company outposts that straddled Lituya Bay at Yakutat and Sitka and massacred those inhabitants they caught. A few colonists escaped. The Russians retaliated by lobbing shells onto native settlements from ships lying safely offshore. They retook Sitka, but there were further revolts.

The increasing number of whites, smallpox, and homemade liquor—the latter being another gift of the newcomers—took their toll on the Tlingits, who could not be defeated by arms. The home-brewed liquor, whose ingredients consisted of whatever was handy at the moment, was called "hooch," or a derivative of that word.[†]

There was a flurry of Russian sea otter hunts in Lituya Bay in the mid 1820s, but the catch had diminished to a few hundred. What sea otters remained were now hunted mainly by the Tlingits, who employed the same deadly techniques as the Russians. They traded the skins for the manufactured goods that they had come to believe were necessities.

Looking back from mid-century, a Russian historian noted: "Sea otters are found in the vicinity of Yakutat and Ltua Bay to

---

[†]There was this account of American trading practices later in the century: "They [the Tlingits] are very fond of coffee, sugar, and molasses, and like all other Indians easily become fond of ardent spirits, to obtain which they will sometimes sacrifice nearly everything in their possession. In this manner they are imposed upon by those who know no principle or law, who have been known to sell them essence of peppermint, Stoughton's bitters, and absinthe, charging them four dollars a bottle (holding one pint). Absinthe is a compound which, if used as a constant beverage, soon unseats the mind, produces insanity, and sometimes death."

the present day, but not in such multitudes as in early days, and besides, the entrance to these bays is very dangerous, so that the Company does not hunt there any more."

American whaling vessels began showing up in increasing numbers, and Russian authorities complained about the behavior of their crews: "Moreover, in their rowdiness they have often demolished native huts and small company posts, answering with threats or derision when reminded of the existing regulations and of the prohibition against whaling near shore. . . . Not many colonial districts were spared such visits, always accompanied by some sort of violence."

From three to four hundred vessels worked the offshore Fairweather Grounds in the months of June and July between 1846 and 1851. A few must have been wrecked trying to gain the entrance to nearby Lituya Bay. Some must also have made it inside to escape storms and seek fresh water and firewood. No written records exist of these activities, nor would such private enterprises want to divulge their inner workings to potential competitors.

Then, for a moment, history was obliterated by the first giant wave known with any certainty to come roaring out of Lituya Bay and spill its contents—be they humans or manmade or natural objects—into the gulf.

Sometime between mid-August of 1853 and early May of 1854, a wave, originating near the head of the bay as a huge splash, swept the shoreline to a maximum height of four hundred feet during its mad plunge toward the gulf. It swept inland for a half mile at a low point along the shoreline. The erosive power of the wave was far greater than what was needed to instantly reduce a living human to a spare skeleton or completely denude a thick cedar of all branches and bark.

Such a wave would have certainly destroyed the Tlingit villages seen by Lapérouse near the entrance; and, in fact, there was a story about such a village being wiped out at about that time. A woman who was picking berries on a hillside was the lone survivor.

The date was determined by counting the annual growth rings of a large cedar that grew just above the devastation. The tree had been damaged, possibly by debris, on the side facing the bay. There were one hundred rings outside the injury to the two-hundred-year-old tree, from which a section was cut in 1953. Don Miller of the U.S. Geological Survey wrote: "The assumption that the injuries were caused by the wave was convincingly confirmed by the many similarly damaged trees found along the trimline of the 1958 wave."

Miller, who also used old photos to determine wave heights, thought the 1853–54 wave had been caused by an earthquake that generated a rockslide at Mudslide Creek on the south shore. The highest point of the wave was directly opposite on the north shore, that being the flank of the same ridge that was denuded in 1958.

The initial wave subsided to an average height of eighty feet—double what was needed to qualify it as a mountainous sea—as it careened from shore to shore of the narrow bay. This wave came closer than succeeding ones to matching the destructive power of the 1958 wave, and it marked the end of effective Russian control of the region.

CHAPTER VI

THE AMERICANS.

ALASKA CHANGED HANDS IN 1867, and the governance of its indigenous peoples deteriorated further. Where before there had been laws, rules, and customs accumulated over one hundred and twenty-six years of Russian hegemony, now there was no effective government or law enforcement. Chaos ruled, and the Tlingits were its victims.

The German ethnologist Aurel Krause, who spent six months among the Tlingits fifteen years after the transfer of sovereignty, wrote:

> A new spirit moved in with American possession which destroyed that individuality of the native tribes which had up to that time been fairly well maintained. The Russians who lived among the natives adapted themselves to their customs and habits of living so that, as Vancouver remarked, they differed little from them. The Americans, on the other hand, who now poured into the country to seek their fortunes, concerned themselves very little about the customs of the Indian population and pursued their own purposes with no consideration of them even when they lived in blockhouses in their midst as traders and prospectors.

History is in the pen, or word processor, of the particular scribe. The naturalist and U.S. Treasury Department agent Henry W. Elliott was in Alaska at the same time as Krause. He saw the Russian legacy quite differently. Elliott wrote: "The wild savage life which the Russians led in these early days of their possession of this new land—their bitter personal antagonisms and their brutal orgies—actually beggar description, and seem well-nigh incredible to the trader or traveler who sojourns in Alaska today."

Following the American acquisition of this vast territory, scientists arrived to take its measure. The first American descriptions of Lituya Bay were obtained from a distance, for the entrance to the bay already had a fearsome reputation, and the remote fjord lacked the amenities that might entice visitors.

William Dall was director of the Scientific Corps of the Western Union Telegraph Expedition charged with the ill-conceived task of finding a route for a telegraph line from the United States to Europe via the Bering Strait. The boat that was taking the scientists north passed offshore of Lituya Bay in 1865. "It presents the appearance of a great fissure or rent in the high plateau which forms this part of the coast," wrote Dall. The Western Union scientists had a sense of history, for they named a peak south of the bay Mount La Perouse. Dall would return a few years later and enter the bay.

George Davidson was in charge of a U.S. Coast and Geodetic Survey party that was hastily organized in 1867 to chart the coast while the negotiations for the purchase of Alaska were under way. The party was onboard the revenue cutter *Lincoln,* and matters of navigation took second place to rescues and attempts to control the arms and liquor trades. The *Lincoln* also passed off shore of Lituya Bay. Davidson drew on existing accounts for the description of the bay in the first edition of the *Coast Pilot of Alaska,* published in 1869.

Relying heavily on Lapérouse's journal, Davidson cited the narrowness and danger of the entrance and said it was best entered at slack water—low tide slack for a sailing vessel and either tide for a steamer.[†] Once inside the bay, Davidson wrote: "No sound but the fall of great masses of ice disturbs the silence of this terribly grand but gloomy gorge."

Some Tlingits still inhabited the bay on a seasonal basis, there being a small settlement on the south shore where the French had handled the shaman's remains. A trail led north for two or three miles to a Tlingit fishing camp.

Later editions of the *Coast Pilot* were more narrowly focused, but in this first edition Davidson, who drew his impressions from "a comparatively short and late season," did not hesitate to state how the Tlingits should be governed: "Uniform kindness, strict justice, prompt decisions, and rigid execution of purpose are the corner-stones of any policy by which they can be humanely governed." Davidson returned to Alaska in 1869 and then became a professor of astronomy, geodesy, and geography at the University of California.

In the following decade, Dall headed another government surveying party, which spent four summer seasons along the gulf coast gathering material to update the first edition of the *Coast*

[†]Directions in succeeding editions of the *Coast Pilot* have varied over the years. Local fishermen believe the tide tables published by the government are inaccurate for Lituya Bay. The trick is to determine when the current changes. That will indicate slack water and a ten- to twenty-minute window of opportunity. High tide slack is now preferable for all types of vessels.

Pilot. They entered Lituya Bay on May 15, 1874, and spent the next five days there.

The captain of their schooner, the *Yukon,* was Edward P. Herendeen. He was familiar with the bay, having commanded a whaling vessel four years earlier that had passed through the entrance in search of deserters who had made off in a whaleboat. Herendeen did not know that they had been killed elsewhere by the Tlingits.

Dall noticed what would come to be recognized as evidence of a giant wave; but he did not know of, or even suspect, the existence of such an unusual phenomenon.[†] The coast survey assistant employed the methodology of rational deduction, which did not fit the reality of the place.

From observing the floating glacial ice in summer, Dall deduced that the bay froze solid in winter. (Not true.) When the ice began to break up, ice dams were formed at the entrance, "backing up the waters of the bay behind them, as drift and evidences of flooding and washing were observed along the shores ... to a height of at least ten feet above the high-water mark," he observed. Had Dall been aware of the giant waves, the "flooding and washing" would have been a perfect fit.

Dall regarded Lituya Bay with a mixture of awe and trepidation. He referred to the mountains as "the magnificent sierra-wall of alps" and thought the Saint Elias Range "includes the

---

[†]There may have been another giant wave during the interim, or it could easily have been debris left over from the 1853–54 event. Don Miller wasn't sure. He thought there was a tree line in photographs that suggested a wave midway between 1854 and 1899.

highest uplifts yet known on the North American continent."
Down the precipitous slopes that surrounded the bay "five or six
glaciers fall in true ice cascades to the water's edge." The bay was
"a sort of Yosemite Valley . . . with its floor submerged six or
eight hundred feet." He concluded: "The scenery is grand."

Danger lurked at the periphery of magnificence, however:

> At the narrow entrance in rough weather the breakers,
> except at slack water, extend clear across and in moderate
> weather there are breakers on both spits. . . . In perfectly
> calm weather the incoming tide shows a bore of consider-
> able magnitude and the same is true with the first part of
> the ebb, especially when the wind is from the southward.
> It is only practicable to pass through the entrance at slack
> water. Once in the tide-way, the vessel is carried through
> instantly as if sailing down hill.[†]

The language is reminiscent of Lapérouse, and a footnote accompanying this passage mentions the loss of the twenty-one
sailors in 1786. Indeed, the French explorer was very much on
their minds: "To him is due much of our knowledge of the bay,"
Dall wrote in the 1883 edition of the *Coast Pilot*. The surveyors
named La Perouse Glacier and Mount D'Agelet, the latter after
the noted French astronomer who accompanied Lapérouse.

[†]Dall called the waves at the entrance "a bore or tidal waves." A bore is
a wave or a set of waves caused by the sudden onset of the flood current up
a narrow estuary or river. A tidal wave is a misnomer for a tsunami, since
no tide is involved. Dall was confronted with a new phenomenon and was
at a loss for words and an appropriate concept to describe it.

The party set up an astronomical observatory on La Chaussee Spit and then warded off the Tlingits who sought to board the *Yukon*. The natives were well armed and fortified with home-brewed liquor. Fortunately, there were no violent incidents.

The surveyors set about determining the heights of the nearby major mountain peaks. The position of the entrance to the bay on most charts was found to be erroneous. Lapérouse's chart of the inner bay "was tested," Dall said, "and proved to be generally accurate." Dall did not mention changes in the locations of the glaciers since the time of Lapérouse, which meant that either there had been none, or he did not explore the end of the bay.[†]

The Tlingits were seasonal occupants of Anchorage Cove on the north shore. They resided in "a few temporary huts." All that remained of the village near the entrance on the south shore were "a few tombs of wood." They found no evidence of the cenotaph that Lapérouse had erected on the island nearly ninety years earlier.

As testimony to the thoroughness of Dall's navigational work, the third edition of the *Coast Pilot* in 1891 remained virtually unchanged from the previous one. It was this edition that was used most extensively, because it was available during the frenetic gold rush period. And Dall's sketch of the entrance to Lituya Bay, a masterpiece of clarity (see the title page of this book), was included in the 1950 edition of the navigator's bible.

[†]Twenty years later a party from the Canadian Topographical Survey, working on a determination of the international boundary, found that the glaciers in both arms had advanced about three miles since 1786.

Dall, whose name was given to numerous animal and marine species in Alaska, visited the territory in 1895 after retiring from the survey.[†] The Smithsonian naturalist related his impressions in a speech given later that year to the Philosophical Society of Washington. "The state of the law is uncertain, the seat of authority is obscure, divided illegitimately between naval officers, the revenue cutter service and a powerless governor.... The day of the ethnological collector is past. Southeastern Alaska is swept clean of relics; hardly a shaman's grave remains inviolate."

THOSE PERSONS charged with law enforcement, meaning the crews and officers of revenue and naval vessels, were the greatest desecraters of the dead. Cheap transportation was a necessary ingredient in the economics of the trade.

One of those naval officers and grave robbers was Lieutenant Emmons, an occasional visitor to Lituya Bay on board two patrol vessels. It was Emmons who termed the bay the most feared harbor on the Pacific Coast. He added that "the constant warfare of the ocean waves and tidal currents have formed a bar over which the rollers break with terrific force, and, except in fair weather, at slack water, the passage is fraught with extreme peril."

It was also Emmons who secured the pipe that told the story of Kah Lituya and who sold the American Museum of Natural

[†]Both Davidson's and Dall's names adorn many Alaskan landscape features. In terms of nomenclature, the government men were very kind to themselves and each other. They also favored historical figures like Lapérouse and his associates. It is a miracle that the native name for the bay has survived.

History in New York City more than five thousand Tlingit artifacts between 1888 and 1897.[†] (One hundred years later I would
examine some of those same items in a storeroom on the sixth
floor of the museum.)

Altogether, Emmons would sell more than eleven thousand
objects of Tlingit art and everyday use to such museums as the
Smithsonian, the Field Museum of Natural History in Chicago,
Harvard's Peabody Museum, the Thomas Burke Memorial
Washington State Museum in Seattle, and the Museum of the
American Indian in New York, where the pipe was acquired.
Artifacts collected by Emmons found their way to museums in
Berlin and Saint Petersburg. The leading authority on the Tlin-
gits, Frederica de Laguna, later wrote: "Through direct pur-
chase from him, or by exchange between institutions, there is not
now a major museum in this country or abroad that does not
have specimens collected by Emmons."

There was a feeding frenzy among museums for Indian artifacts from the Pacific Northwest. Many objects, such as masks,
totem poles, and at least one skull, were taken from villages and
shamans' graves at a time when museum collecting was pursued
in a much less politically correct manner.

Emmons fudged on his methods of acquisition, mostly so that
other collectors couldn't tap his sources. To increase prices, he
played one museum against the other. "It is possible that his ac-
quisitiveness overcame his sensibilities," wrote his biographer,
Jean Low.

[†]One of the more unusual and perhaps private artifacts was a baby boy's
first stool, deposited in a wooden box in the forest by his mother, who de-
sired him to grow up strong and powerful.

His practices and motives were truly despicable, judged by modern standards. There are no clear indications of how he was judged by the Tlingits at the time, although he was supposedly welcomed because of his impressive naval uniform and his unusual interest in their culture.

But it was mainly Emmons's acquisitions that inspired an early appreciation for primitive art in this country. There were shows and expositions in San Francisco, Seattle, Chicago, and New York that featured his purchases. The noted anthropologist Claude Lévi-Strauss was fascinated by them. Through Lévi-Strauss such surrealists as Max Ernst, André Breton, and George Duthuit were influenced by an art form that suggested the world of the unconscious, as explored by Freud and Jung.

Although he lived to the age of ninety-three, Emmons's life was discordant. The son of a distinguished admiral, he ranked near the bottom of his class at the Naval Academy and was considered a poor officer. There is no question, however, that he was an avid collector who used military service to further his own means. With no degree in anthropology, Emmons received the accolades of the profession.

As an amateur anthropologist, Emmons reluctantly wrote a few journal articles on scattered aspects of Tlingit culture, but he could not produce a major work. Of his repeated attempts to write an overarching monograph on the Tlingits, Emmons said in 1898: "I find the work very confusing and attribute my ill health wholly to that cause." He was to struggle with the project for fifty-eight years.

The book was left for de Laguna to complete from fragments remaining after Emmons's death. *The Tlingit Indians,* published in 1991 by the University of Washington Press and the American

Museum of Natural History, was the result. An introduction and biography written by others were appended.

Emmons arrived in Alaska in 1882 onboard the USS *Adams* and transferred two years later to the USS *Pinta* as executive officer. These small gunboats were mainly concerned with law enforcement. While on duty, the lieutenant came across two important items that bore upon the Tlingits' history of Lituya Bay. His account indicates the manner in which these primary source materials were acquired:

> In 1882 upon reaching Juneau at four A.M. in Sept. I was ordered to take an armed boat crew ashore and avert a supposed murder in the Auk village. Having first arrived in the sloop of war *Adams* for two years' service in Alaska, I had no idea in what house in the ranch the man lived or as to his identity so I took the old Chief Kowee and required him to guide me to the house. This was the beginning of friendly relations with "Kowie" who was a very fine old type and some years later in 1886 just one hundred years after La Perouse entered Lituya he gave me the full account of the first meeting of several canoe parties of his Tlingit forebears who were in the bay at that time and their astonishment at seeing the ships and white men and their old legend of the spirit of the tide bore that enters the bay and I later got at Hoonah a large old carved feast pipe that illustrated the spirit. I had a copy of La Perouse with me in Alaska and was familiar with the catastrophe but Kowie's account that had been handed down by word of mouth through a century proved the accuracy of native history and was most interesting.

While Emmons went to unusual lengths for an American officer to understand the culture of the Tlingits, neither he nor the missionaries had any use for the long-haired Tlingit shamans, who practiced a different type of magic and medicine. "Emmons himself was present and may even have taken an active part in apprehending and punishing such shamans, done by publicly cutting off their hair," de Laguna wrote.

Perhaps the shamans retaliated, silently. In an editor's introduction to Emmons's book, de Laguna noted: "The person who approached a shaman's grave or handled his things was believed by the natives to risk serious illness or death." In an article in the *Alaskan Journal,* Low wrote: "Emmons knew of this taboo, yet helped himself many times to the priceless ethnological treasures contained in these forbidden places."

During his Alaskan service, Emmons was plagued by unspecified "ill health" and had to take numerous sick leaves. The Navy declared him unfit for service in 1899. He wrote Franz Boas at the New York museum that year that he had "suffered a complete collapse."

Low commented in the biographical material contained in the book: "Forty-eight years old, ill, and forced to retire, he found his days of active service in the Navy and his residence in Alaska were both at an end. His Navy career, though far from illustrious, had served as a stable base for his career of collecting, far more important to him. He suffered from both psychological and physical ill health and was plagued by recurring bouts of both the rest of his life."

THE TRANSIENT GOLD MINERS arrived in the 1890s. These avaricious seekers after instant wealth damaged the land, the wildlife, and themselves.

The Russians may, or may not, have sporadically mined the placer deposits of gold on the black sand beaches to the north and south of Lituya Bay. The idea that they had was cited in American government reports at the time; but there was never any attribution, and the Russians did not mention such an activity.

The Americans, however, went about attempting to extract the rare metal with a vengeance. At the height of mining there were between one hundred and fifty and two hundred people spread along the beaches. The miners, who both preceded and coincided with the Klondike gold rush of 1897–98, arrived in late spring and left in early fall with little to show for their intense efforts.

The tiny, floury particles of gold, along with minute amounts of platinum, were flushed from the mountains by coastal streams and became embedded in ruby-red sand layers one to two inches thick. Flowing water and mercury, an attractor, were applied to the beach sand in sluice boxes, rockers, and long toms.

To extract the diminutive flakes between storms and other natural distractions was hard work. Grizzly bears were constantly about, clouds of mosquitoes settled on exposed flesh in good weather, rain brought rheumatism, and the wind that either howled down from the icy heights or came straight off the stormy gulf buffeted all with equal violence.

There is this description of placer mining by J. B. Mertie Jr., a government geologist:

> Mining at Lituya Bay is carried on along the beach. It is
> said that 1896 was one of the best years on record, because
> the storms during that year were particularly heavy and fre-
> quent. Yet the miner has to work quickly after a storm, as
> another storm may arrive before he has cleaned up the beach

concentrates and either dissipate or cover them. These conditions make small-scale beach mining an intermittent and uncertain undertaking.

The results were meager, which led to frustration, anger, and murder. From 1894 to 1917, perhaps $75,000 worth of gold was extracted.

Fear and its handmaidens, cruelty and violence, were about. Seals were shot from shore, bears were shot on land, bald eagles were shot in the air, and one hundred and eighty trout were scooped from a lake with a single haul of a makeshift burlap net.

Instant riches were on everyone's minds. There was this story:

"Look at these diamonds," said one miner who held something in his hand.

"Show me you bastard," said the other.

Whereupon the first miner laughingly displayed the glittering eyes of a fish into which he had incised facets.

"I'll kill you," screamed his companion.

A variation on the same theme was related by another miner:

One day I found a dried fish eye in my pocket. Taking my knife, I cut facets around it to make it resemble a diamond, and told the men I had found a diamond. Being mineral-conscious and expecting anything of Alaska, they half believed me. I had to be careful, however, not to let any of them get it into their hands. It was not until half the summer was over that they really knew what I had.

With the increased activity came disappearances, shipwrecks, miraculous tales of survival, and deaths.

In January of 1892 ten miners were stranded in the bay, and Captain Washburn Maynard, with Lieutenant Emmons as executive officer, motored north from Sitka in the dilapidated *Pinta*. The entrance was a stormy mess. The captain decided he would not take the coal-burning converted tugboat through the breakers. He saw some Tlingits on the beach. The *Pinta* repeatedly blew its steam whistle, but there was no response.

Two men got off the coastal steamer in Sitka later that year and told a remarkable story of survival. They had sailed from Juneau in August with supplies for a mining party in Lituya Bay; they misjudged the current at the entrance and their vessel was swept on the rocks by "a revolving current." They swam to shore.

With winter approaching and no desire to spend those dark, stormy months in that place, the men decided to hike the one hundred miles north to Yakutat. They took six days of supplies, thinking it would be a five-day trip. As far as they knew, no one had ever made the overland journey. The trip actually took eighteen days, and the men would have starved to death except for the fact that they were aided by Tlingits, from whom they stole a canoe for the last leg of the journey.

Two years later Hans Jensen, a well-known sea captain in Sitka, brought a prospecting party into the bay. There was a violent storm, and his anchored schooner broke its mooring and was cast upon the rocks. A few weeks later Jensen went hunting in the mountains and wounded a mountain goat. While pursuing the goat, he fell over a cliff. The unfortunate captain lived for a few days and then died.

A few Tlingits still visited the bay in the 1890s. There they crushed berries in a canoe and let them ferment, creating hootch that was exceedingly potent. Ten Tlingits were killed when they got into a drunken brawl amongst themselves.

There were other wrecks and drownings at the entrance to Lituya Bay during the period of the gold rush—too many to mention them all, even if they had been adequately documented at the time. Little was known about the exact fate of the steamer *Discovery*. She was known to be unseaworthy and sank off the entrance in November of 1903 with an undetermined number of passengers and crew that could easily have reached fifty. The Tlingits watched the vessel flounder from the vantage point of the spit.

THE YEAR PRECEDING the end of the century was quite eventful.

It was the year that the chief of the Hoonah Tlingits, Kooghsee, made the following speech to the territorial governor:

> Now not very far from where I live is Lituya Bay, where our people, our ancestors, used to go hunting for sea otters and hair seal. Now that place is taken away from us. Great many schooners going there. White people are there now. These white people, when they make camp, they make lots of smoke. That scares animals, sea otters especially. . . . And when we talk to those white men they say the country does not belong to us, belongs to Washington. We have nothing to do with that ground. All our people believe Alaska is our country.

The Harriman Alaska Expedition sailed blithely past Lituya Bay in the early summer of 1899. The floating Gilded Age university was, in the words of a later Smithsonian Institution publication, "perhaps the most remarkable private expedition of all time." The wilderness historian Roderick Nash said the expedition consisted of "the foremost scientific, literary, and artistic talents in the country." Another way to put it would be to say that never had so much talent and brains been rented for two months by one American.

Nearby Alaska was considered exotic, but safe, thus making it an ideal destination for such a group. The railroad tycoon Edward H. Harriman chartered a steamer and, at his expense, filled it with fourteen members of his family, twenty-five of the most celebrated scientists in the country, and assorted artists, photographers, taxidermists, stenographers, and what not. The ship was stocked with multiple cases of champagne and a five-hundred-volume library, mostly dealing with Alaskan matters.

The passengers included William Dall of the Smithsonian, by that time regarded as the dean of subarctic explorers; the naturalists John Burroughs, John Muir, and C. Hart Merriam, the latter being chief of the U.S. Biological Survey; the publisher and ethnologist George Bird Grinnell; the geologist and glaciologist Grove Karl Gilbert, after whom one of the inlets in Lituya Bay was named; the chief geographer of the U.S. Geological Survey, Henry Gannet; and the Seattle society photographer Edward Curtis, who would go on to photograph Indians in the Southwest.

There were high jinks, learned discussions, bruised egos, some research, and the plundering of Tlingit villages of artifacts, such as totem poles.[†] The Victorian members of the expedition, trav-

---

[†]The expedition stopped at Cape Fox, a small Tlingit village that had been temporarily abandoned. The crew labored a full day to dig out and float a half-dozen of the best totem poles to the ship, from where they were transported to the California Academy of Sciences in San Francisco, the

eling in the splendid isolation of the two-hundred-and-fifty-foot steamship *George W. Elder* were oblivious of the condition of the Tlingits and many other realities of Alaskan life at the time.

The expedition stopped in Sitka, where George Emmons, newly retired from the Navy, showed the distinguished visitors Tlingit artifacts not normally seen by outsiders. They rowed ashore to gaze at the towering face of the La Perouse Glacier and then passed Lituya Bay, where thick clouds obscured the mountain heights. They explored Yakutat Bay and then departed on June 23rd, touching the Siberian coast briefly before heading back.

On the return trip, they passed offshore of the Fairweather Range in the afternoon. Muir, no slouch when it came to appraising mountains, wrote in his journal that "the Fairweather Range was absolutely cloudless, and glowed in its robes of snow and ice with ineffable beauty and glory of light. . . . This is the grandest range, the richest in sculpture, with infinite gables and V-shaped valleys and canyons."

Merriam hurried to the other side of the ship, where Harriman and his wife gazed from deck chairs upon an empty ocean.

"You're missing the most glorious scenery of the trip," said Merriam.

"I don't give a damn if I never see any more scenery," growled the multimillionaire, who was in a hurry to get back and run his railroads.

Field Museum in Chicago, the Peabody Museum at Harvard, and the universities of Michigan and Washington. Expedition members entered the empty houses and removed artwork, and grave markers were taken from the cemetery. It was not science's finest hour.

Three months later a huge earthquake, greater in magnitude than the 1906 San Francisco temblor, struck Yakutat Bay and its environs.

As far as Lituya Bay is concerned, the September 1899 earthquake is one of those black holes of history. Little is known with certainty about what occurred there, although a giant wave once again scoured the bay's shoreline to a maximum height of two hundred feet in Crillon Inlet. Most probably the wave was caused by a landslide in the inlet. Perhaps five Indians were drowned on Cenotaph Island and a native village and fish saltery were destroyed near the entrance. The beaches were clogged with uprooted trees torn from the forest by the destructive force of the wave.

At the time there were numerous miners in and around the bay, but no detailed accounts of the earthquake and wave in Lituya Bay emerged.[†] A seemingly thorough report on the earthquake was published thirteen years later by the U.S. Geological Survey; but it focused on the events in Yakutat Bay, and there was no mention of Lituya.

There were reasons for Lituya Bay's omission in the report. Tlingits were not noteworthy. The scientists confined their field

---

[†]There was a reference to the giant wave, or waves, in a Juneau newspaper that hinted at a massive rearrangement of the beach just north of Lituya Bay and explained why the 1900 mining season would be a bust: "Last fall Alaska was subject to earthquake shocks. These were accompanied by tidal waves which either sucked the gold bearing sands into deep water or cast boulders and rocks upon the beach to a great extent. Whatever happened, the shore is piled four feet deep with a mass of rock which the sea will have to remove as the expense of clearing away the mass of material is too great to consider."

observations to Yakutat Bay, and when they sent out six hundred questionnaires asking for descriptions of damage, all went to the mailing addresses of governmental agencies and businesses. No such entities resided in Lituya Bay, nor was there any post office.

What transpired at Yakutat Bay in September, however, could have easily taken place in nearby Lituya Bay and is worth recounting on its own merits.

Two parties of prospectors, totaling eight men, were camped astride the Fairweather Fault on Disenchantment Bay, an arm of Yakutat Bay thirty miles distant from the village. There had been constant earthquakes. The prospectors rigged a makeshift seismograph consisting of dangling hunting knives that emitted a wind-chime noise when they jiggled.

Fifty-two foreshocks were counted on September 10th before the big shake. The shoreline instantly rose between seven and forty-eight feet; elsewhere it sank beneath the waters of the bay. The prospectors were thrown to the ground or clung to tent poles while the ground shook violently for two to three minutes.

One prospector later recalled:

We ran from our tents, leaving everything behind. . . . In the course of five minutes the Hubbard Glacier, five miles across its face, ran out into the bay for a half a mile. . . . This lake broke from its bed and dashed down upon our camp while we ran along the shore and escaped its fury. Everything went before it or was buried by the thousands of tons of rock that came down. This deluge was almost immediately followed by one from the sea. A wall of water twenty feet high came in upon the flood from the lake and carried all debris back over the undulating morainic hills.

Another prospector described the scene in the following manner: "We heard a terrible roar in the direction of the bay, and on looking that way we saw a tidal wave coming toward us which appeared to be about twenty feet high and was preceded by some great geysers shooting into the air, some of which were several feet across and thirty or forty feet high."

This tumult understandably unnerved the men. The senior author of the government report, Professor Ralph S. Tarr, commented on the situation:

> Threatened thus from both front and rear by waves and floods, with the ground trembling beneath their feet, and the thunder of crashing bergs and avalanches in their ears, it is small wonder that the prospectors ran to and fro aimlessly, not knowing whether to run to the high land first or to return to their tents for some of the provisions and blankets which were threatened by the waves.

That night the men huddled in the rain. They tore strips of clothing and bound themselves to small saplings so that they would not be shaken loose. Fearsome noises surrounded them on that Walpurgisnacht: the crack of disintegrating glacial ice, the roar of landslides, the thud of huge boulders tumbling in swollen streams.

Daylight brought a means of escape. A damaged Tlingit canoe was floating in the fjord. They brought the large canoe ashore, patched it, and loaded a few provisions aboard. As on a polar expedition, they had to portage across large masses of ice that had been shaken loose from the glaciers. Three days later they arrived in the village, where they found the frightened residents camped on what became known as Shivering Hill.

There had been a series of giant waves. "The entire Yakutat Bay Inlet was thus swept by at least one great water wave," wrote Tarr. The northern tip of Khantaak Island dropped into the gulf, as it would again in 1958.

The effects of the earthquake were widespread throughout the Northwest. At Lake Chelan in Washington State, twelve hundred miles to the south, twenty-foot waves were set in motion and a small boat was cast ashore. Tarr wrote: "The writers [of the report] have seen no description of a region being shaken longer, more vigorously, or more continuously, even in Italy, Japan, or Formosa, since the beginning of the seismographic recording of earthquakes. For four weeks the earthquakes were to be counted by the hundreds and on four or five days world-shaking disturbances took place." [†]

IN THE SAME MONTH as the earthquake, Hans and Hannah Nelson arrived in Lituya Bay. The couple unknowingly provided the ingredients for a human drama that would parallel in kind, if not extensiveness, the recent natural acts of violence. The Nelsons had been lured to the bay by promises that could not possibly be kept. But how were they to know?

The promises were contained in the widely distributed prospectus of the Latuya [*sic*] Bay Gold Placer Mining Company

[†]Professor Tarr of Cornell University died suddenly in his Ithaca, N.Y., home at the age of forty-eight while working on the final proof sheets of the USGS professional paper, which was published later in 1912. He had been a frequent visitor to the Gulf of Alaska coast during the previous decade.

that failed to mention waves or drownings or earthquakes or, for that matter, anything questionable about the bay. It was depicted as a wild Eden that could easily be tamed, where riches could be effortlessly plucked from the sands.

The stock offering had all the aspects of a scam. Company officers came from New York City and California, where the firm had offices in San Francisco. On a map depicting railroad and steamship transportation routes supposedly linking Lituya Bay and San Francisco, both places were shown in the same-sized type. The company's twelve hundred acres of mining claims extended north to Cape Fairweather. A one-hundred-and-sixty-acre town site was designated on the bay.

The prospectus recalled Lapérouse's glowing commercial expectations, the only difference being that gold instead of furs was now the principal inducement. A large factory or factories would be constructed there to refine the gold. There would be a town with wharves extending into the bay. The climate was mild. Timber, water, salmon, wild game, and wild berries, enough of the latter to support a cannery, were plentiful. Potatoes, turnips, parsnips, radishes, lettuce, and cabbage could easily be grown in the "naturally irrigated" soil. There was no mention of winter.

True, there had been no bonanza at Lituya Bay, yet. But this was because "crude and unminerlike" techniques were being employed. Still, as much as $40 a day could be extracted by a single person. Much more could be taken out with "the best and latest improved mining machinery," which, of course, the company would willingly provide, at a cost. "At a low estimate, many millions of dollars worth of the precious metal are stored in our claims," said the prospectus.

The company gave a small "button" of gold, supposedly from Lituya Bay, to the superintendent of a California mine. The superintendent wrote, "I will say if the sample is an average one, then you have the biggest fortune ever dreamed of."

The superintendent's letter was displayed prominently in the prospectus. It took a careful reading of that document to determine that the five owners of the California mine were the major backers of the Lituya Bay venture; the superintendent, therefore, had a vested interest in deception.

The prospectus concluded that the company owned the "most extensive and most promising" placer claims in the Northwest and would be "honestly managed on business principles."

The Nelsons bit, along with at least three other miners—Fragnalia Stefano, Sam Christianson, and M. S. Severts. The five were to continue working the claims and act as caretakers for the company during the long winter months of 1899 and 1900, when most miners left the region.

Nelson was a large Norwegian (some said a Dane) who had a good sense of humor. He was a carpenter and the foreman of the mining crew. His wife, an Englishwoman, was small and quiet but full of spunk. She had been a domestic servant. They may have met in Chicago.

The couple and the three miners lived separately but took their meals together in the Nelsons' cabin next to either Justice or Echo creek, the exact location north of Lituya Bay not being clear from contemporary accounts.

The log cabin, just a few hundred feet off the black sand beach, was a world apart from that open terrain. The thick undergrowth of devil's club and ferns, over which towered a dense overstory, enclosed the occupants in a wet crypt. The liquid oppressiveness of the darkening fall months bore down upon all.

They were eating dinner in the cabin on October 6th when Severts got up and went outside. The others continued eating and talking.

A few minutes later Severts returned, leveled a .45-caliber Colt revolver at Stefano, and shot him dead.[†] He then swung the weapon around and fired at Christianson. The bullet struck a stone jar and creased the flesh of the miner's neck. He fell to the floor in shock.

Severts next aimed the weapon at Mrs. Nelson. Her husband jerked Severts's hand down, and the bullet tore into the killer's leg, where it left an ugly wound.

Mrs. Nelson choked Severts with a dish towel while her husband tied him up.

It was over in a few minutes; then they had a wounded murderer to guard for the remainder of the long winter.

They found his packed valise outside the cabin. When asked if he had attempted the killings for the $800 in joint earnings, "maybe" was Severts's enigmatic answer.

At this point accounts began mentioning "miners," indicating a wider involvement than just that of the Nelsons in what eventually transpired. There were other mining claims in the area, and the company may have had more than one caretaking crew. Mining law evolved from codes adopted at mass meetings, and civil and criminal matters were handled similarly in remote mining camps.

[†]Some accounts say a .38-caliber revolver, others a double-barreled shotgun. In any case, it was not a trifling weapon.

A passing steamer was hailed but did not stop. Tlingits were hired to carry Severts to a cabin closer to the bay and guard him. After a few weeks the Indians, who did not relish being implicated in the white man's affairs, refused to mount guard duty. That left no alternative but to attempt to observe the proprieties.

The miners conducted a trial, and Severts supposedly confessed to planning to kill his four companions for the small amount of gold. His festering wound was torturing him, and he begged to be killed. It was not clear from local newspaper accounts who exactly hanged Severts from a tree on the north end of La Chaussee Spit. Such matters were usually joint affairs.

When the coastal steamer docked at Sitka in May of 1900 with news from the north, the local newspaper noted: "The *Excelsior* also reports a lynching bee at Lituya Bay. Two men were murdered there last fall and, it being impossible to communicate with the authorities at Sitka and fearing to set the murderer at large in the community, being satisfied of his guilt, the Lituyans thought it proper to take the law into their own hands, hence the elevation of the criminal."†

Lynchings, although not uncommon in the history of the West, were apparently a rarity in Alaska. A study of criminal justice found no other reported lynchings in the state's history.

Christianson recovered to become a popular beer-wagon driver in Juneau, where he frequently told the story of the shooting. The Nelsons, who were exonerated of any wrongdoing, dabbled in mining and operated a general store in Atlin, British

---

†The original newspaper story mistakenly had two miners killed. I have followed the more trustworthy account subsequently published in *The (Sitka) Alaskan* of October 13, 1906.

Columbia, before retiring to Bellingham, Washington. The La-tuya Bay mining company faded from sight after encountering numerous difficulties, not the least of which was a lack of gold.

Jack London wrote a story, "The Unexpected," that was based on this incident. It was cribbed from an exaggerated account of the murder/lynching that ran in the lurid Sunday magazine of William Randolph Hearst's *San Francisco Examiner,* an exem-plar of the era's yellow journalism. The headline, designed to strike terror in male readers, read: "Woman Hangs a Man And the Law Upholds Her." An accompanying drawing showed Mrs. Nelson decked out in her Victorian finest, demurely hold-ing a hanging rope in her gloved hand.

London neatly paired the strengths and weaknesses of the two sexes. Hans was paralyzed by the enormity of killing a man. Hannah had the strength to pull a barrel out from under Severts. She then had an emotional breakdown and had to be helped away by her husband. He concluded the story on a melodramatic note: "But the Indians remained solemnly to watch the working of the white man's law that compelled a man to dance upon the air."

The famous author made the mistake of labeling this fictional account as true. In *Jack London and the Klondike,* the scholar Franklin Walker observed: "The trouble with the story, how-ever, is that it once more illustrates the adage that truth is stranger, and less plausible, than fiction. The actual event remains quite incredible, even if it really took place, and the story based on it suffers in consequence."

One of the problems of written history, or what represents it-self as the first draft of history, meaning in this case a newspaper account and London's subsequent magazine story, is the tyranny of the printed word. The Nelsons, and others, came to believe London's version of the events.[†]

THE FIRST TWO DECADES of the new century were a time of transition for Lituya Bay. Gold mining tapered off, and a handful of draft dodgers made the bay their temporary home during World War I. A government surveyor arrived to take stock of strategic minerals. He did not find the iron and platinum needed for the war effort, so he departed, and the population declined further.

The geologist Mertie visited the bay for three days in 1917. He reported: "The mouth of Lituya Bay is a narrow entrance, beset with rocks and shoals, through which the tide runs with a velocity of ten knots or more; and unless the ocean is more than ordinarily calm the sea breaks clear across the entrance." He quoted extensively from Lapérouse's journal, the Frenchman still being the written authority on the bay.

[†]Like Bohn, I came across a note inserted in the Alaska State Library's copy of the August 1906 issue of *McClure's* magazine that contained London's story. A Juneau resident, Mrs. M. B. Keller, had met the Nelsons on the boat to Seattle some years after the incident. Mrs. Keller's short note stated that Mrs. Nelson said London's account was correct. Bohn took this as confirmation. I don't. I believe that Mrs. Keller wanted to believe that it was true, or Mrs. Nelson found it more convenient to say it was so, or Mrs. Nelson had come to believe what the general public had been told, or some combination of the above. Mining and journalism practices at the time, along with the few scattered contemporary references to the incident, have convinced me that the better story is not true. By such calls, made by Bohn and myself and others, is history fixed. The oral tradition of storytelling allows for greater flexibility in such cases.

Mertie was credited with the discovery of the Fairweather Fault: "This depression [Desolation Valley], with little doubt, represents a great fault rift, which may perhaps continue for considerable distances northwest and southeast of the ice-filled valley just described." He thought the rapid advance and retreat of the glaciers surrounding the bay were "due mainly to earthquake action, which is common in this district." Mertie missed the indications of a giant wave, which must have been fairly fresh. They were spotted thirty-five years later by another government geologist.

Around this time a few people gave some thought to living in this unforgiving region. There were two types of settlers; those who survived and those who died. An example of the latter was V. Swanson, whose diary was found in his cabin north of Lituya Bay by two trappers. Extracts follow:

Oct. 4th, 1917: Getting sick packing, now looking for camping place. Cold in the lungs with a high fever.

Oct. 27th: Shot a wolf and a bear cub.

Oct. 28th: Winter has come. Strong wind, two feet of snow.

Nov. 18th: Finished one fur coat of bear, wolf, and lynx.

Nov. 22nd: Left eye bothers me. Shot one goat.

Dec. 7th: The wind is so strong that you can't stand upright. River froze except a few riffles. Too much snow and too rough for sleighing. Snow getting deeper now.

Dec. 25th: Very cold. A good Christmas dinner. Snow getting hard. River still open in places above camp.

Feb. 1st, 1918: Cold weather nearly all month of January. Lynx robbed my meat cache up river. Salt and tea but once a day. Gradually getting weaker.

Apr. 1st: Got to the house with what I could carry. Wolverines have been here eating my skins, robes, and moccasins, old meat, and also my goatskin door. They tried to run me [out] last night, came through the stovepipe hole showing fight. Heavy fall of snow. Canoe and some traps down the river about five miles, close to Indian grave mark. Camp about half way.

Apr. 3rd: Still snowing. Cooking my last grub, no salt, no tea.

Apr. 12th: Seen a fox track today. Birds are coming too. Fine weather.

Apr. 15th: The no-salt diet is hitting me pretty hard. Eyes are getting worse, in the bunk most of the time.

Apr. 20th: Finest weather continues again, cooking my last grub, got to stay in bunk most of the time—my legs won't carry me very far. My eyes are useless for hunting, the rest of my body also useless. I believe my time has come. My belongings, everything I got I give to Joseph Pellerine of Dry Bay; if not alive, to Paul Swartzkoph, Alsek River. April 22, 1918. V. Swanson.

Lituya Bay's first and only settler, at least of European descent, was a hermit.

Jim Huscroft was a survivor. He arrived between 1915 and 1917. Huscroft once said that he was from Steubenville, Ohio, where he had made and lost three fortunes, but that reply was invented to quiet a persistent questioner. What was certain was that he had found a place that fit his needs.

Huscroft was shy and elusive. A stocky, powerfully built man with a sad-kindly round face, bald on top and heavy-jawed below, Huscroft always greeted visitors who arrived by boat or floatplane at his dock with a pocket watch in hand and the question: "I make it out to be [such and such a time]; what do you make it?"

He was alone for long stretches of time, mostly in the winter. In the summer, Huscroft was deluged with visitors. His kindness, generosity, and hospitality were legendary along the coast.

One visitor recalled that when he arrived during the depths of the Depression years there was not the customary ritual of comparing time, but rather the following lament:

> "Say it ain't so, Bob, say it ain't so."
> "What ain't so, Jim?"
> "That the kids in New York City is eatin' out of garbage pails. I've been thinking about it all winter. There's all those salmon in the bay and goats in the hills, an' if I could just get some cans I could help some. Tain't right for kids to be eatin' that way, you know, an' I want to help 'em out. Been thinkin' about it all winter."

His home was on the west side of Cenotaph Island. There Huscroft built a comfortable L-shaped cabin, with a hardwood floor of birch, and numerous outbuildings. He had a vegetable garden and also raised foxes, whose pelts were the latest in women's fashions. Most of the foxes ran free on the island, which served as a natural pen. A pet fox, named Tuffy, came up to the back door at each meal to be fed, and another perched on his broad shoulder.

There was a small dock off which his boat was moored. Huscroft fished, trapped, and did a little prospecting in the bay and along the coast in both directions. His was a shipshape operation.

Huscroft was a man of habit, and every morning he cooked enormous sourdough pancakes. Snuff was a basic necessity; he always had a plug of it under his upper lip.

Once a year he hitched a ride on a passing boat to Juneau. The hermit became seasick and frightened when the boat passed through the entrance. In Juneau he loaded up on his favorite salted mackerel and snuff and other essential supplies, drank copious amounts of factory beer, picked up his mail at the post office, and collected the previous year's newspapers, saved for him at the Elks Club.

Back at his island home, each morning Huscroft read the newspaper that had been published exactly one year earlier while eating his customary huge breakfast. He never looked ahead to determine the resolution of some issue: "It don't matter which year it is. The news is all the same anyway," said Huscroft. "Only if I peeked ahead, it'd take away the fun."

Huscroft loved the solitariness of that place. He developed the habits of a recluse. His money—a considerable amount, it was said—was kept in a cigar box secured by a rubber band. He talked very little, just scraps of thoughts uttered aloud and then completed in his head.

The climax of the year for Huscroft was Christmas dinner, which he planned and executed in lonely splendor. He picked the wild strawberries, blueberries, and salmon berries. He canned the vegetables and made home brew. When the time was right, he shot the wild goose. Then he sat down all alone and ate roast goose, vegetables, and a variety of pies.

But the world began to intrude. Salmon cannery executives who flew the coastline kept caches of fuel for their seaplanes at the bay. Occasional parties of trappers and prospectors dropped in to take a quick look around. Commercial fishermen who worked the offshore Fairweather Grounds used the bay for a harbor of refuge.

Then, beginning in 1930, the sport of mountain climbing descended upon Lituya Bay and Jim Huscroft in the form of the summer presence of privileged Ivy League college boys who were looking for a dry roof and some of the hermit's famed pies.

While waiting out a storm in the snug cabin, the boys heard the hermit recite his favorite ditty:

> Little drops of water,
> Coming down as big as your fist,
> That's Lituya Bay Mist.

It was a bit like the Hardy Boys discovering China. Huscroft was from another planet. This was the story the Harvard boys related to explain who Jim Huscroft was:

> All of the gang was sitting around the cabin one rainy day talking about Harvard. It was the one word being mentioned most frequently.
>
> Jim got one of the climbers aside and asked him, "What the hell is this Harvard anyway?"
>
> The gang thought that was great. Not where is it, but what is it.[†]

[†]The story reveals more about the teller than the person whom it was being told about. What was Harvard, anyway, in comparison to Lituya Bay?

Those boys were a charmed bunch. The climbers went about their business upon the mountain heights that decade and somehow managed to escape unscathed. They were fleeting presences in the bay. Dave Bohn, who participated in the first ascent of Mount Lituya in 1962, wrote: "For we were just passing through on our way to the mountains beyond, with no intentions of leaving behind the mess usually found after men (climbers and mountaineers included) defile the wilderness with their garbage."

The Harvard University and Dartmouth College expeditions were all led by Bradford Washburn, an instructor in geographical exploration at Harvard. When the Harvard expedition of 1930 first entered the bay in a rickety vessel, the current was so strong and the engine so weak that the water spun the boat around, and they entered backward. The seven climbers only made it halfway up 15,300-foot Mount Fairweather.

No climb was more dramatic than the first ascent of Fairweather in 1931.

Allen Carpé, a noted New York mountaineer, led a four-person expedition that had planned to land at Cape Fairweather. After ten days of stormy weather on their boat ride from Juneau, they were forced to come ashore at Anchorage Cove in Lituya Bay.

On the hike north along a beaten path that paralleled the coast, the group, with the addition of two Russian trappers who helped carry supplies, encountered the remnants of the gold mining era. "The woods are full of decaying sluice-ways, tumble-down cabins and rusting equipment disintegrating before the inexorable advance of the wilderness," Carpé wrote. "Today the region is deserted. Twenty miles down the coast Lituya Bay, a

beautiful harbor with a narrow and difficult entrance, is the natural base for operations."

After two months of hiking, bushwhacking, crevasse hop-
ping, and dodging numerous avalanches in unmapped terrain,
Carpé and Terris Moore, who would later become president of
the University of Alaska, reached the summit. They were com-
plimented by the London editor of the *Alpine Journal* for "a
magnificent expedition" that was "the hardest yet accomplished
among the 'Arctic' mountains of North America."

Another Harvard expedition returned in 1932. In 1933 a
Harvard-Dartmouth expedition combined scientific research
with mountain climbing. After coming within 340 feet of the
12,726-foot summit of Mount Crillon, the climbers descended to
Huscroft's cabin to await their departure date. Robert Bates, one
of the climbers, recalled:

> We had just finished a salmon supper in Jim's cabin, and
> Bradford Washburn was proudly holding up a heavily iced
> cake we had baked in Jim's oven, when the door opened and
> in came six gaunt, bearded men. They were five Dutchmen
> and a Finn who had been prospecting and run low on food.
> When they saw the cake, our one cake of the whole sum-
> mer, their eyes lit up. It turned out they had been living on
> bear meat for the past week and were sick and tired of it.
> We filled them up on salmon and beans before cutting
> the cake.

A few moments after they had polished off an apple pie and
an orange-frosted cake for dinner on August 30th, 1933, there
were two sharp jolts. The hanging lamp swayed; the attached

shed pulled away from the house. Jim told the college boys that earthquakes were a frequent occurrence in the bay.

A Harvard-Dartmouth expedition reached the summit of Crillon in 1934. Washburn wrote an article explaining the difficulties of climbing in Southeast Alaska, as compared to the Alps of Europe:

> Most Alpine ascents start at four thousand, or even five thousand, feet, and then, usually, the next three or four thousand are covered in a funicular or aerial tramway.
>
> To climb the peaks of the Fairweather Range one starts by wading waist-deep in seawater, unloading supplies in the surf. There are no trails through the thick lower forests. The glaciers which are usually veritable highways in the Alps, are for the most part honeycombed with crevasses hidden under a thin, treacherous blanket of winter snow and blocked by stupendous icefalls. There are no huts, no porters, no guides, and no fresh food.
>
> Mountaineering in Alaska is still little short of Arctic exploration, with all of its attendant difficulties and hardships. But the beauty of the country casts a spell which is well-nigh impossible to shake off.

The lowlands, through which the climbers had to tramp, were a mysterious place:

> Little is known about the Fairweather Peninsula, even in Alaska itself. At Juneau, a hundred miles to the east, prospectors and boatmen tell fabulous tales of the enormous patches of wild strawberries which line its western beaches, the terrific tide rips at the mouth of entrancing Lituya Bay, of sparkling glaciers dropping headlong to the sea, and of vir-

gin forests draped with Spanish moss, dark and mysterious as the jungles of the Tropics.

Accompanying Washburn's story, which appeared in the March 1935 issue of *National Geographic,* was a photograph of a suspender-clad Huscroft standing in his garden with a plate of newly dug potatoes in one hand. When Huscroft went to town the next fall on his annual trip, stacks of mail awaited him from readers. There were recipes for jam, questions about what it was like to be a hermit, and seven marriage proposals. A badly frightened Huscroft beat a hasty retreat to his island.

PRECIPITATION FOR THE MONTH of October 1936 was far above normal for southeastern Alaska. There was more rain, hail, thunder, and lightning during the predawn hours of October 27th; or it was clear. Accounts varied. It was that kind of place.

Two fishermen, Nick Larson and Fritz Frederickson, were on board the thirty-eight-foot trolling boat *Mine,* anchored off Fish Creek on the north shore. They heard a loud, steady roar beginning at 6:20 A.M. The fearful noise continued for half an hour.

The fishermen saw a steep wall of cresting water, perhaps one hundred feet high, extending across the head of the bay at 6:50 A.M. They were under way and in deeper water when the first of three waves raised their small vessel fifty feet into the air and then dropped it close to the bottom of the bay. Huscroft's seine boat, anchored nearby in fifty feet of water, actually touched bottom.

The second and third waves, each successively higher, passed underneath at about two-minute intervals. Smaller waves sloshed back and forth for a half hour. Broken trees and pieces of glacial ice floated on the bay.

Huscroft and a guest, a young man by the name of Bernard Allen, who was seeking adventure, heard a roar coming from the mountains. It sounded like "the drone of one hundred airplanes at low altitude," said Allen.

Jay Williams of the Forest Service visited the bay shortly after the waves and gathered the following account from Huscroft, who said he was preparing breakfast at the time:

> He was suddenly startled by a terrifying roar much louder and more ominous than the usual artillery-like booming and cracking of the near-by glaciers to which he was accustomed. Rushing outside he was appalled by a sight comparable to the one which must have met the gaze of the children of Israel when the Red Sea rolled back. It appeared as though all the water in the bay was rushing out to the entrance in one mountainous tidal wave. Spellbound and uncertain for the moment he hesitated long enough to see an immense back wave, the reaction of the initial rush of water dammed by the heavy ocean swells and the narrow bay entrance, seeking to restore the normal water level. Jim said that his dominant thought at this moment was to reach the highest ground on the island and that he started for it at no lingering pace.

They ran up the trail that led to a spring, which furnished the cabin with running water through an iron pipe.† The older man watched the tumult through the trees. The waves demolished

_____

†I would find the spring and pipe forty-four years later, and it would furnish me with water on the otherwise dry island.

one of his outbuildings and lifted another up and set it down far inland. Luckily his main cabin, which was on higher ground, was only flooded. Huscroft's boat was not damaged.

There was a considerable loss, however. The laboriously accumulated topsoil in his garden was washed away, and the vegetables spoiled in his flooded root cellar. Huscroft faced a bleak winter.

The young man returned to Juneau on the next available fishing boat.

Don Miller later determined that the biggest wave had reached a height of four hundred and ninety feet along the northeast wall of Crillon Inlet. From the head of the bay, successive waves rebounded toward the gulf at lessening heights, reaching as far inland as two thousand feet along the lower reaches of the bay. Near the entrance to the bay, crabs and clams were found half a mile inland. A few days later the trunks of trees washed up on beaches fifty miles to the south of Lituya Bay.

The geologist was never able to find a suitable explanation for the 1936 waves. There was no earthquake or earthslide, nor was there any release of ice-dammed water from above. Miller also discounted the falling meteorite theory of another scientist. He thought "some kind" of sudden movement of the Crillon Glacier was to blame but could not determine the exact cause or the source of that continuous roar.

HUMAN TRAGEDIES continued to abound.

One year after the waves, two greenhorns from the Midwest showed up in Lituya Bay, where they planned to trap that winter. Jay Williams encountered them and pointed out that jumping trap lines was not regarded as a friendly act in Alaska. They agreed to move to one of Huscroft's cabins north of the bay, where a diary was found later that winter.

Williams recalled in his book, *Alaskan Adventure:* "They were practically out of food and without snowshoes. Trapping had been very poor and the diary stated that they would try on the morrow to reach Lituya Bay with their skiff if it looked at all favorable. They said they hoped to obtain a larger boat from Jim and move their belongings to the island inside Cape Spencer. That was the last ever heard of them."

The three waves of 1936 sapped something inside Jim Huscroft. His health began to deteriorate. He complained of rheumatism, a not uncommon affliction in that moist environment. His foxes died of the mange, and the cabin and vegetable garden fell into disrepair. He did what little needed to be done in order to avoid starving to death and seldom strayed off the island.

When the small coastal freighter *Patterson* was wrecked on the beach north of the bay in the winter of 1938, Huscroft—ever the good Samaritan—hobbled painfully a few miles north along the coast to leave a note and a cache of food at one of his cabins for the stranded crew, who were later rescued by the Coast Guard.

A concerned friend stopped at Huscroft's place and persuaded the old man to go to Juneau with him on board his boat, named the *Cenotaph.* As Huscroft passed through the entrance to the bay for the last time, there were tears in his eyes.

They put into a small harbor to wait out a storm, and it was on board the boat that the hermit died on March 23, 1939, at the age of sixty-six. Washburn made sure that a cenotaph was erected in Huscroft's memory on the island.

CHAPTER VII.

THE WAVE.

————

WITH THE DEATH OF HUSCROFT and the ascendancy of Glacier Bay National Monument under the management of the National Park Service in the 1930s, the human history of Lituya Bay went into a precipitous decline. The bay dropped from sight during World War II and the immediate postwar years. It was as if one continuous fog bank obscured that place and did not begin to lift until 1952. For the next six years there was a gradual emergence; then the bay shook itself mightily in 1958, and the world took brief notice.

On June 6, 1952, a young geologist who was working for the U.S. Geological Survey's oil investigation program in the gulf arrived in Lituya Bay. Don J. Miller poked around for a few days. He found the hermit's cabin, which he made his base camp. It was in fair shape.

He noticed the difference in the trim lines. Then Miller talked to the fishermen whose vessels were anchored there. They told him of the giant waves that had periodically swept the bay. The geologist was caught by that place—to the point of obsession.

Miller had graduated with a master's degree in geology from the University of Illinois and gone to work in Alaska for the survey in 1942. He was a serious person, dedicated to his work, organized, methodical, and a keen observer with a logical mind.

He was extremely strong, a quality that contributed to his being quite capable in a wilderness situation. A photograph shows him standing with his face cast down in an introspective mood. Miller was a loner and close to nobody except his family.

Miller returned to Lituya Bay in the summer of 1953 for a three-week stay. He camped on the island and at the mouth of Topsy Creek, a few miles south of the bay. He resumed his work, which was to map the oil-bearing strata, but at the same time he doggedly pursued the matter of the giant waves. He cut sections from trees and gave them to the Forest Service Research Center in Juneau. A tree-ring count disclosed that there had been a disruption in 1936 and another in the 1853–54 growing season.

Miller reported his preliminary findings at the Seattle section meeting of the Geological Society of America in March of 1954. He asked his fellow scientists what they thought generated the giant waves. He dismissed other causes, like a glacially dammed lake suddenly emptying, and guessed it was earthquakes; but he had no proof.

To be in the right place at the right time for a rare movement of the earth is the fervent wish of all geologists. It becomes a reality for only a few. Miller was one of the chosen ones. He thought his destiny had been fulfilled.

After flying over Lituya Bay the day following the 1958 earthquake and noting the wave's elevation at 1,800 feet, Miller returned to Glacier Bay.[†] He listened to a radio interview with Bill

---

[†]The altitude was later corrected with a handheld altimeter. The tree line was at 1,720 feet, but there was unmistakable evidence that water had sloshed through the forest up to the 1,740-foot level.

Swanson, one of the surviving fishermen, and accounts by others of a cataclysmic event of its type unmatched in history.

THE LONG SUMMER EVENING was clear and an oily swell undulated across the surface of the gulf as three fishing boats headed toward the calm entrance of the bay to anchor on the night of July 9th. The *Edrie* was first into the bay at 8 P.M. On board were Howard Ulrich and his son, Howard Jr., nicknamed Sonny.

They were tired after a long, unsuccessful day trolling for salmon. Ulrich was tempted to anchor in the lee of Cenotaph Island but instead selected a cove on the south shore about one mile from the entrance. He was in a contemplative mood, and the black-legged kittiwakes on the south end of the island were unusually raucous, filling the bay's still air with their piercing cries of *kittiwake, kittiwake*.

Father and son ate dinner, washed the dishes, and then settled down in their bunks. Another long day of fishing lay ahead of them, or so they thought.

Just before falling asleep at 9 P.M., they heard a boat's engine. It was the *Badger,* with Bill and Vivian Swanson on board. The Swansons headed toward the end of the bay to get some glacial ice and then reversed course and put their hook down in Anchorage Cove.

At about the same time, the *Sunmore* entered the bay and anchored just behind the spit, about halfway between the *Badger* and the entrance. Orville and Mickey Wagner, a young couple who had purchased the *Sunmore* a few months earlier, were friends of the Swansons. The couples exchanged waves. The Juneau fishing community was a tight-knit group of people who looked out for each other on the high seas.

As the last two boats entered the bay, a climbing party of ten Canadians departed. They were the first Canadians to have successfully climbed Mount Fairweather, whose summit is bisected by the international boundary. British Columbia's centennial was that year, and a Canadian Broadcasting Corporation television crew had accompanied them partway up the mountain. Their base camp was on the beach, close to where the Swansons anchored.

The exhausted climbers had returned earlier that day from the long trek down the sterile heights, across the Fairweather Glacier, and along the coast. Their expedition had taken two weeks. They took long baths in the nearby freshwater lake, collected souvenirs, such as sea urchin shells, and relaxed in the momentary peacefulness of the lush surroundings.

The expedition was scheduled to leave the following day, but the pilot of their Royal Canadian Air Force amphibian arrived at 6 P.M. that night and told them to pack immediately. He was worried about the possibility of fog and wanted to get the climbers safely back to Juneau that night. The climbers cursed the pilot's nervousness. They missed dinner in the hurry to pack and departed at 9 P.M.

Another party of ten climbers was due that day by boat, but they had been delayed. Some of their supplies had already been delivered to Huscroft's old cabin, which would serve as their base camp. Had the two groups proceeded as planned, there would have been a total of twenty climbers camped on the shoreline of the bay that night.

As the Canadian climbers flew away, so did the nervous black-and-white kittiwakes. The gulls ascended like so much confetti blown upward. The high-intensity alarm call of thousands of birds echoed through the still bay. They passed over the *Badger* and splattered the boat with droppings. Some crashed into the vessel's rigging and plummeted to the deck. The Swansons were frightened.

Just before the earthquake another fisherman noticed the birds squatting on the black sand beach north of the bay, as if they were waiting for something. Not all the kittiwakes escaped. Afterward, the bodies of gulls littered the shoreline of the bay.

The gulls of Lituya Bay were not the only wildlife exhibiting strange behavior that evening. Some Yakutat families were fishing in the Situk River and picking berries nearby when they noticed terns and other small birds suddenly taking flight. The birds circled in the air and made frantic cries. Each cast hooked a fish shortly before the earthquake. The wildflowers trembled from foreshocks.

IT WAS SUNSET in the high latitudes when the earth shook and the land was ripped apart at 10:16 P.M. When it was over—some three or four minutes later—the earth had moved 21.5 feet horizontally and 3.5 feet vertically at one point along the fault line.[†]

The land danced, as did everything upon it. One mountain peak rose fifty feet in an instant. The tip of Khantaak Island in Yakutat Bay sunk one hundred feet beneath the water, sucking three berry pickers to their deaths.

All that remained of the outing were the paper plates that floated upon the roiled waters and a mangled outboard motor-

---

[†]The greatest horizontal displacement in the 1906 San Francisco quake was twenty feet. The shaking lasted one minute. The periods of shaking for the ruinous 1989 Loma Prieta/San Francisco and the 1994 Los Angeles quakes were measured in seconds.

boat belonging to the berry pickers. The sides of the fiberglass hull had been compressed and the cabin sheered off, but flotation within the hull had kept it afloat. The three bodies were never found.

The Yakutat postmaster and his wife had left the island just moments before. Glancing back, they saw a wall of water obscure their friends and the trees on Turner Point. Going twenty-five miles per hour, they could not have outrun the wave. By the time it reached them, however, the wave had diminished greatly in the deep water. Witnesses on land said the bay "looked alive" and was "heavy, dark, and boiling."

Nature was turned upside down.

What looked like ocean swells rippled across the land. Sand blows and water geysers erupted eight feet into the air. Fissures snapped open and closed like giant clam shells. Rivers rocked like cradles, flowed upstream, or were blocked temporarily by ice dams formed from collapsing glaciers. Downstream flows lessened and then surged when the temporary dams gave way.

There was a deep, continuous rumbling from the very bowels of the earth, a phenomenon that accompanies many earthquakes. A putrid, sulfur-like smell from long-decayed organic matter was released from the fractured ground and settled over the landscape.

Wildlife was stricken: coyotes howled, grizzly bears fled, bull moose broke their horns in panic-stricken flight through the forest. In the water, whales became airborne and shellfish and barnacles were swept from their rocky underwater perches, their attachment plates neatly severed in the process.

Lituya Bay was a charnel house of nature. Fish rotted on shore and the bloated carcasses of mammals floated upon the surface of the water. Marine plants withered on land, and fresh-water plants atrophied in the salt water.

For humans, the quake was no less devastating.

Ulrich was awakened by a deafening roar. The water around the *Edrie* began to vibrate. The stoutly built thirty-eight-foot boat seemed to jump out of the water. Ulrich looked toward the mountains in the waning light and saw them smoking from avalanches.

Then he saw the huge wave, perhaps one hundred feet high at the outset, then diminishing in height as it caromed down the sides of the bay.

"Christ, it looks like the end of the world in here," he yelled into his radio microphone.

Other fishermen heard him and stopped their chatter.

"The noise is terrible and it looks like there's a fifty-foot tidal wave heading toward me. It's a solid wall of water coming at me. I'm going to try to head into it and see if I can ride up over the top of it."

Then another hurried transmission: "Mayday. Mayday. This is the *Edrie* in Lituya Bay. All hell has busted loose in here. I think we've had it. Good-bye."

In the single photograph that I have seen, Ulrich, a solidly built man in his thirties, has one large hand on the shoulder of a smiling seven-year-old Sonny, who has both of his hands in his pockets. They look like true partners. Their boat was strong and graceful. The three seemed like a unit that functioned together smoothly. They would need all of that solidarity.

When Ulrich first saw the wave, he remained rooted to the deck. Then he moved fast. He threw a life jacket on Sonny and started the engine while putting out his call for help.

He tried to haul in the sixty-four-pound anchor with the power winch. It would not budge, so he let the anchor chain out to its two-hundred-and-ten-foot limit and maneuvered the boat so that it was pointing into the oncoming wall of water.

The wave was cresting as it sped by the north end of the island, but on the south side it had a smooth face some fifty or seventy-five feet high. It pushed the boat back and lifted it upward. The anchor chain snapped.

Ulrich looked down and saw trees underneath the *Edrie.* The wave carried the boat over the shore and then back into the bay, where Ulrich turned it about to face the backwash that rebounded from the shoreline.

Other fishermen heard him say: "It's awful."

Time passed slowly.

"Well, we rode to the top of it. We got over the top okay."

A confused sea with high, steep waves of twenty feet or more buffeted the boat as Ulrich made for the center of the bay. Large chunks of glacier ice, each a veritable iceberg, and huge tree trunks flowed on the strong ebb current toward the *Edrie,* threatening to entrap it and pierce its thin skin.

The fishing boat *Lumen* arrived off the entrance to the bay and Stutz Graham, Ulrich's radio partner, asked if he should come in and help.

"No, for Christ's sake don't come in here. Stay out."

The listening fishermen, concerned about the deadly waves at the entrance, gave Ulrich advice.

"There's big trees, branches, leaves, roots, and everything, everywhere I look. All around me. I've got to get out of here. I never saw anything like it. I've got to get out of here."

One fisherman pointed out that the current in the entrance was at its most dangerous stage, and Ulrich's boat might be swamped in the breaking waves.

Instinct told Ulrich to flee.

"The big timbers are closing in all around me. I have to get out. I'm heading toward the entrance. This looks like the end of everything. I don't know if I can make it, but I can't stay here. I have to get out. I'm heading toward the entrance."

"We're right in the middle of the entrance."

"We made it. We're on the outside."

It was 11 P.M. Their ordeal had lasted forty-five minutes.

The Wagners were not as fortunate. The *Sunmore* was last seen by Swanson heading toward the entrance. It was picked up by the giant wave and hurled over Harbor Point, where it disappeared from sight. An oil slick marked the young couple's watery grave. Like those of the French sailors and the three berry pickers, their bodies were never found.

The Swansons also felt their boat vibrate. They looked out the door and saw the side of a mountain collapse into the upper end of the bay. Then they saw the cresting wall of water heading toward them.

"As it came up out of the deep water and hit the shallow water, then it just piled sky high. It just seemed like it grew about fifty feet right there near the entrance. And it was just a matter of seconds later that the base of the wave hit us, and that popped the cable," said Swanson in the radio interview.

The boat rose and kept rising to a point where it was eighty feet above the trees on the spit. It was hurled stern-first, like an out-of-control surfboard, over the spit. There was a horrible crash in the gulf at the end of the wild ride, and the boat began to sink.

Huge trees were landing all about like so many spears. One came through the door and hit Swanson in the chest, driving him toward the stove. The tree exited the mortally wounded boat the same way it entered, leaving Swanson with four broken ribs.

The couple clambered into their eight-foot skiff with only their underclothes on. It was a cold night, and when the wind came up it became chillier. They were seized with cramps.

They heard an engine. A searchlight swept the water but missed them. The boat disappeared, reappeared, then disappeared again. The couple cried for help. Mrs. Swanson passed out. Her injured husband was just about to give up.

It was shortly after 11 P.M., and Graham and an exhausted Ulrich were searching for survivors in their separate boats. About a half hour later, Graham and his son decided to make one more sweep through the area on the *Lumen.*

The Grahams saw a light on shore and headed toward it. It was described as a "small flickering light" in the notes of Diane Olson, who monitored the radio transmissions that night on board the fishing vessel *White Light,* thirty-five miles from Lituya Bay.

Graham cut the engine and drifted in order to hear better. There was a plaintive cry. He turned on his searchlight. The cry was louder. The Swansons were found huddled in their half-sunken skiff in a direct line between the *Lumen* and the mysterious light.

They were taken to a Juneau hospital, where Swanson was interviewed. He recovered quickly. Vi Swanson's hair changed color from brown to white that night. It was the last time she went fishing with her husband.

Ulrich and his son continued to search for the Wagners until 5:30 A.M. They were exhausted and headed home to Pelican Bay. Ulrich's boat went aground exactly one year later. He repaired the *Edrie* and floated it off on the next high tide. Shortly thereafter, Ulrich gave up commercial fishing.

MILLER RETURNED VIA HELICOPTER to Lituya Bay for a one-day visit in early August and then came back for a three-day stay later that month. He took no chances and located his campsite at the peak of the two-hundred-and-ninety-foot hill on Cenotaph Island. With him was Don Tocher, a seismologist from the University of California at Berkeley.

They heard rumbles from the head of the bay and small waves lapped at the shoreline, but Miller was disappointed. "Nothing unusual," he wrote in his field notes.

On September 2nd they flew back to the Bay Area and began to reconstruct what had happened on July 9th from the accounts of eyewitnesses and the scientific evidence writ so large upon the landscape.

Beginning at 10:16 P.M., the west side of the fault moved northwestward and upward in a series of violent lurches. There was churning along the entire one hundred and fifteen miles of the Fairweather Fault from Palma Bay northward to Nanatak Fiord. The epicenter was forty-five miles southeast of Lituya Bay in Cross Sound. The moment magnitude, a more accurate measurement for large quakes than the Richter scale, was 8.3, compared to the 7.7 magnitude of the 1906 San Francisco quake.[†]

[†] In terms of amplitude, the shaking was four times greater in 1958 than in 1906.

The gigantic temblor was felt nine hundred miles to the south in Seattle, where twenty musicians in a floating orchestra pit bounced up and down for five minutes. In Whitehorse, Canada, one hundred and eighty miles to the east, there was panic in a movie house and two water mains burst. Submarine cables snapped between Skagway and Juneau, and the quake was felt in Anchorage, four hundred and seventy miles to the northwest.

Rockslides and avalanches tore down the mountains surrounding Lituya Bay. Clouds of rock dust and snow rose into the air—the smoke that Ulrich saw. Not less than one minute nor more than two and a half minutes after the first shock, the flank of an unnamed 5,616-foot peak on the east side of Gilbert Inlet was shaken loose and plunged en masse into the head of the bay—the falling mountain that Swanson saw.

The noise was deafening. The violent impact of forty million cubic yards of rock, ice, and coarse soil weighing ninety million tons—an amount equal to eight million medium-duty dump truck loads—was heard fifty miles to the north. Ulrich said it sounded like "an explosion."

The resulting surge of water wiped the trees off the granite spur of the opposite ridge. The splash wave had tremendous force, a conservative estimate being twenty-five million foot pounds of pressure. (Only three hundred thousand foot pounds of pressure are needed to uproot a tree.) Trees were instantly severed at root level and stripped of all their bark and branches by a force far greater than that used to peel logs at a pulpmill.

A giant gravity wave with a steep front surged outward and, supplemented by the splash wave that washed over the spur, slammed into the steep cliffs near Mudslide Creek. A slide tore down the two-thousand-foot heights, adding to the chaos of the moment. The combined wave sped down the bay at up to one hundred and thirty miles per hour. Four square miles of Lituya Bay's shoreline were stripped of all vegetation, leaving the bedrock exposed and bleeding.

There were more than two hundred aftershocks. The ocean beaches ten miles on both sides of the entrance to the bay were littered with ice and the flayed trunks of trees. If someone had needed rescuing, there would have been no place for a floatplane to land.

There was massive shoaling. Between the island and the south shore the bottom became two hundred feet shallower. An oceanographer with the U.S. Coast and Geodetic Survey concluded that there had been "considerable instantaneous deposition . . . from earth shocks and huge water-wave stripping."

Fortunately, the fantasy of Lapérouse and others of a commercial settlement in the bay had not materialized. Miller noted: "Few works of man existed in Lituya Bay at the time of the 1958 wave, but judging from the effects on the vegetation and the boats, the wave would have wreaked enormous destruction on ordinary buildings and on shore structures such as docks."

There was nothing left of Huscroft's cabin except for a few scattered utensils. The unmanned lighthouse on concrete piers at Harbor Point was no more. Equipment left by a mining company on the south shore had vanished, and most of the brass survey markers set in concrete by the U.S. Coast and Geodetic Survey disappeared.

After the 1958 wave, the Park Service abandoned plans to establish a permanent ranger station in the bay. Although Miller calculated that a giant wave occurred about every quarter century, he estimated that the odds of it occurring on any single day were nine thousand to one.

The wave became the subject of academic conjecture.

Such a wave and the resulting destruction were theoretically possible. A scale model was constructed by Robert L. Wiegel, a civil engineering professor at the University of California at Berkeley and an expert on oceanographic engineering. To generate such a wave, he said, the slide needed to fall quite fast and as a single unit. Wiegel added: "It is a well-documented fact that waves with large energy content are generated impulsively by such varying mechanisms as underwater seismic disturbances, islands exploding, atomic bombs, and large masses of water added suddenly to a body of water."

The first indication that the wave might be an unprecedented event was a small item published in the October 1958 issue of the *Bulletin of the Seismological Society of America,* edited by Tocher: "The water wave in Lituya Bay was perhaps the most remarkable wave on record."

Others soon recognized the uniqueness of the verified height of the wave. Eliott Roberts of the U.S. Coast and Geodetic Survey, writing in the May 1960 issue of the *U.S. Naval Institute Proceedings,* termed it the highest wave known to oceanographers, the previous record being the one-hundred-and-twelve-foot ocean wave encountered twenty-five years earlier by the U.S. Navy ship in the North Pacific.[†]

[†] In oceanographic literature, the Lituya Bay wave is called a splash, surge, or impulsively generated wave. There are also wind-generated waves in the open ocean and *tsunamis* (tidal waves) caused by earthquakes. The

That same year Miller published his findings about the giant waves in a U.S. Geological Survey professional paper titled *Giant Waves in Lituya Bay Alaska.* A shorter version ran in Tocher's seismological publication. Advancement in the federal agency was dependent to a great extent on publication. Miller had reached the pinnacle of his short career.

POSTSCRIPT FOLLOWED POSTSCRIPT, for an event of such magnitude never truly ends. It continues to reverberate, like the aftershocks following an earthquake, through history.

Two titanium prospectors, who had met the Canadian climbers on the trek up the coast, were worried. They flew over what had been the site of the base camp on the shore of the bay the day after the wave and reported that it had vanished. The leader of the centennial expedition, Paddy Sherman, later wrote: "It was the sort of shattering climax which, had it torn some other range asunder, would have convinced the natives forever that their gods were angry because the peak was climbed."

A member of the climbing party that failed to make it into the bay, on being informed of the missing cabin that would have been their base camp, said: "If we'd been on time, I guess we'd have gone, too."

Lituya wave was twice as high as a splash wave caused by a landslide in Italy's Vaiont Reservoir in 1963, when heavy rains caused a slope to give way, and approximately two thousand people were drowned in nearby villages. A similar type of wave only thirty-three feet high killed fifteen thousand people along the shoreline of Shimabara Bay, Japan, in 1792. The fjords of Norway, so similar to Lituya Bay, have been the site of many such destructive waves.

Miller drowned in 1961 while on a field trip with a young as-sistant in southcentral Alaska. Their bodies were found not far from their overturned yellow raft on the Kiagna River by the bush pilot who had dropped them off a few days earlier and later flown back over the area to check their progress.

They were lying below a canyon on separate sand bars along the glacial stream. Those who knew Miller wondered about the circumstances of his death, for he was experienced and able, and the river did not pose any unusual difficulties. Why was it, they asked, that both men drowned? There were no answers.

Miller's stature was such within the survey that the federal agency named one of its Alaskan research vessels the *Don J. Miller.* The vessel was used to study the effects of the giant tsunami that struck southern Alaska after the Good Friday earthquake of 1964.

In a new boat, purchased with the contributions of fellow fish-ermen, Bill Swanson and his brother-in-law reentered Lituya Bay on May 26th, 1962. It was the first time he had been in the bay since the night of the giant wave.

Swanson died of a heart attack shortly after passing through the entrance to the bay. He was fifty years old, had been fishing for nearly thirty years, and had no known health problems.

An archeologist and two field assistants from Washington State University arrived in Lituya Bay in the summer of 1965 to conduct an archeological survey for the Park Service. They quickly determined that there were no sites remaining in the bay. Robert E. Ackerman, the archeologist, wrote: "The scene that greeted us when we arrived at Lituya Bay was one of deso-lation. All the inhabitable area around the shoreline of the bay had been swept clean as if by some giant hand."

They made camp in Anchorage Cove. On the first night a fierce storm from off the gulf blew down their tents. They moved further inland and then began their survey. Using bear trails, they walked south to Steelhead Creek, where they found a decaying log cabin that had probably belonged to miners. Beside it was the large skull of a whale.

Next they hiked north along the beach to Justice Creek and encountered the remains of more mining misadventures, some as recent as the early 1960s. These were the artifacts they discovered: dishes, mason jars, rusting cans, sand-nicked whiskey bottles, generators, a donkey engine, boilers, empty fuel barrels, a truck, a jeep, a bulldozer, log cabins in varying states of disrepair, and more recently constructed tent platforms.

They returned to their camp and prepared to depart. Then the furies struck. "Before leaving Lituya Bay we were treated to a well-developed gale which lashed up the water into towering waves," Ackerman reported. "The small boat that we had left 'safely' anchored in Anchorage Cove was ripped from its moorings and dashed against the jumble of logs that line the shore. Lituya Bay thus struck again."

CHAPTER VIII.

THE PRESENT.

————

SINCE THE GIANT WAVE OF 1958, an average of one fishing boat a year has been lost at the entrance to Lituya Bay. The most recent victim prior to my visit was a forty-six-foot crab boat named the *Sonora Sue*. I saw the remnants of the fiberglass hull wedged in the boulders on La Chaussee Spit, much like raw flesh caught between the teeth of a grizzly bear. The haunting presence of such a carnivorous animal came to dominate my visit to the bay.

Enough with reading books, I had thought; time to go there and experience the place. I did so with great trepidation. History can be a light presence, if one is not personally involved. It could also be a weighty backpack on an internal trek through time.

I needed to solve three problems before I could depart.

It would be a costly trip, what with the flight to Juneau, a hotel stay, and then the chartered floatplane to and from Lituya Bay. I would also have to buy provisions.

I already possessed certain necessary items, such as the easily transportable two-person kayak that I had used before in Glacier Bay and elsewhere. I could ship it as excess baggage on the commercial flight, and it could be stowed on the small plane and then assembled on the beach. I owned a tent and all the necessary camping gear.

I was then the western editor of *Audubon* magazine, and I proposed a story on the bay to Les Line, the editor of that nature publication. He added the idea of a story on a World War II battle fought against the Japanese on Attu, the island furthest west on the Aleutian Island chain and now a national wildlife refuge. Fine, I thought, an Alaskan summer to be financed by someone else.

The second problem was whom to take, for I did not want to venture alone into that bay. There was really only one choice, and that was my son, Alex, now fourteen years old.

We had traveled through Alaska and the American West together. One trip down the Colorado River within the Grand Canyon in wooden dories had been a memorable experience. Other times we had backpacked in the Sierra Nevada, skied in Colorado and New Mexico, and car-camped in Baja California.

With his mother, who worked for an airline, Alex had been around the world several times. They had survived the sinking of a ferryboat off Hong Kong, mostly because Alex spotted where the life preservers were stored shortly before the ship collided with another vessel. They jumped from the listing ferry into the South China Sea and swam to a nearby lifeboat.

He was, in my view, the complete kid.

Was there a risk to him? I didn't think so. In fact, I thought his youth and innocence would protect him from that dark place and perhaps rub off on me as well. Alex would be my good-luck charm and the white shield behind which I would cower. At the same time, he would be looking to me for protection. How ironic.

The last problem was what to do about bears. There were probably more large brown bears (grizzly and brown bears being the same) in and around Lituya Bay than anywhere else in Alaska.

Bear stories were legion. Jim Huscroft had seen as many as nine grizzly bears feeding at one time along the shoreline of the bay. The hermit had distinguished five distinct types of bears: a huge brown bear, a normal-sized grizzly, a small cream-colored grizzly, the common black bear, and a blue, or dun-colored, glacier bear.

Male grizzlies, *Ursus arctos,* are the largest terrestrial carnivores in the world. Weighing between six hundred and twelve hundred pounds, they love fresh meat, charge at forty-two feet per second, and can crush a cow's skull as easily as I can break an eggshell.

There were stories of maulings and close encounters with bears in the national monument. I was aware that at almost the exact spot where Alex and I had spent the first night camping on our kayak trip through Glacier Bay, an Illinois man had been attacked by a young grizzly one month later. The man's bare skeleton, with one hand and boots left intact, was found a short distance from his camp.

After talking with Huscroft in 1937, Jay Williams of the Forest Service went for a stroll in the woods and encountered a large, aging brown bear. Both froze, and then, said Williams, "the bear suddenly whirled and lunged off the trail directly into the forest. Before going thirty feet he smashed his head on into the trunk of a large wind-thrown spruce tree. The impact was so hard that it set him back on his haunches and must have given him a headache, but he soon disappeared in the woods." It was good to know, I thought, that confrontations with grizzlies could be humorous.

Opinion among old Alaska hands on the best bear weapon was divided between a large-caliber rifle, like a .357 Magnum, and a sawed-off twelve-gauge shotgun loaded with slugs. More recently, .44-caliber Magnum revolvers had become the less burdensome, and less accurate, weapon of choice. Two armed persons, at least one having had previous experience with large bears, was the optimum pairing.

I had had brief encounters with harmless black bears while backpacking in the West. Although a Cold War Army veteran who had served on the East German border, I had chosen not to carry a weapon while a newspaper correspondent in Vietnam. I decided not to buy a gun, preferring instead a loud whistle, banging on a tin cup, and my own lusty, off-key singing voice to warn bears of our harmless passage.

The only other baggage that I carried was in my mind. At that time I did not know all the details of the history of Lituya Bay, but I was aware of the general outline. There seemed to be a continuum.

THE TWO OF US set off again for Alaska in June of 1980. On arrival at the Juneau airport, we immediately boarded a commercial flight to Gustavus, where the visitor center and Park Service headquarters for Glacier Bay National Monument were located.

Although Lituya Bay was a very small part of the national monument, what eventually would become a large national park had its genesis there. President Woodrow Wilson withdrew three hundred and twelve square miles from the public domain that surrounded Lituya Bay during World War I to protect the spruce trees for construction of airplane frames. As it turned out, the trees were not needed for the war effort.

A 2.5-million-acre national monument, which took in Lituya Bay, was created in 1925 by President Calvin Coolidge. The centerpiece was the glaciers surrounding the inner bay, celebrated by John Muir and others. During the early years, the Forest Service handled administrative matters, such as leasing Cenotaph Island to Huscroft.

There was little control over or thought given to activities on the wild outer coast, regardless of whether the Forest Service or Park Service administered it. The virgin spruce and hemlock forests surrounding Lituya Bay were a tempting source of revenue for the Forest Service. A bill passed by Congress in the waning days of the 1936 session opened the national monument to mining. Miners hacked a road for a Model TT Ford truck through the brush on the old path to the diggings north of the bay.

A survey from the air by the Park Service determined there were few brown bears in Lituya Bay. "Bears indeed were there in droves," the miners on the ground reported.

The Park Service, during one of its rare patrols of the outer coast in the mid 1960s, counted fifty fishing boats in the bay at one time. The prospectors had made a mess of the shoreline.

Congress designated the monument a 3.2-million-acre national park in 1980; but such an official act meant little on the remote outer coast, and it certainly did not affect our visit.[†]

On arrival in Gustavus, we pitched our tent in the campground near the visitor center. I did some research in the library

---

[†]All the land surrounding the bay and Cenotaph Island were officially designated wilderness. No campground, visitor center, or ranger station would be built there. It was not until 1992 that the Park Service mounted anything resembling an effective patrol of the remoter regions of the park. That year it acquired an airplane to control poaching "of some of the largest specimens of brown bear left in Alaska" and the rarer glacier bear.

at park headquarters and readied our gear. As prearranged, the chartered floatplane arrived on the third day. The mountains were buried in clouds, so the pilot took the sea-level route via the coastline. We picked up wisps of fog near Cape Spencer, the fog bank thickened, and the pilot turned back.

Two days later, the sky was clear. We flew over Glacier Bay, where we had paddled four years previously, and headed toward a low point in the Fairweather Range. It was the same route that Miller had taken twenty-two years earlier.

The mountains, truly one of the world's great alpine sights, glittered with new snow. The jeweled white expanse was blinding. Huge, gaping crevasses creased the extensive glacial plain. We descended and joined the coast at the point where the La Perouse Glacier calved directly into the gulf, then headed north.

The plane banked to the right and approached the bay from the ocean. The first thing I noticed from the air was that the tidal current was inbound. A white-flecked V was engraved upon the water at the entrance. We passed over the same flood current that had sucked Lapérouse's two ships into the bay.

As the floatplane skimmed over the water preparatory to landing, I made out the devastating haircut the 1958 wave had given the bay. Crowded along the shoreline, just above the highest of the high tides, were the bleached remains of tree trunks, many still attached to their severed roots. They resembled the jumbled piles of weathered bones from a holocaust of unimaginable proportions.

The plane pulled up to the beach on the west side of Cenotaph Island, that being the location I had selected for our base camp. Like Huscroft, I thought there would be fewer bears on the island. The west side was also more protected from the chill

Arctic winds that blew from off the frigid glaciers, and there was a view of the densely vegetated coastal strip.

We were busy for the next few minutes unloading the equipment and supplies. The bush pilot and I briefly confirmed the arrangements for his return in eight days, and then he started the engine and was off.

Alex forlornly watched the plane depart. He never liked that place. It gave him the creeps from first to last. That independent-minded young man stuck to me—especially when bears were around—like the duct tape I used to repair my knee-high rubber boots.

WE HEADED TOWARD THE TREES to look for a place to pitch our tent. The day was warm; the sun was hot. Yet as soon as we climbed a low bank and entered the forest, a coolness descended.

A short path led to a campsite, most probably used by Park Service rangers, I guessed, during their infrequent visits to the bay. A tarpaulin was strung over a picnic table and a tent was pitched on a wooden platform.

I wondered who could be here. Inside the tent there were two cots separated by a metal footlocker. Books, a lantern, and field notes were scattered about. The reading material and notes suggested scientific researchers of some type.

Alex called out, "Hey, Dad, I'm hungry."

"Okay, kid, give me a few minutes to figure out what's happening here."

Above the picnic table I saw a wooden box, retrievable by pulleys and a rope, that served as a bear-proof food cache. Into the box went our food. I found a flat spot for our tent with a view of the bay a short distance from the established camp. Alex wanted to sleep closer to the others, whoever they might be, but I thought that would violate camping ethics.

We ate our lunch quietly at the table. The bay was still. The view through the trees was a perfectly framed picture of The Paps. The strait and the long flat spit were also visible. The backdrop for the history I had absorbed was now displayed before me on a panoramic scale.

THAT AFTERNOON, with Alex's help, I assembled the kayak. I secured it with a long line to a tree—a precaution, albeit a feeble gesture should there be a giant wave.

We walked along the beach, skipped stones on the still bay, had the first of many thumb-wrestling matches, and found a creek in which there was a trickle of water. That would be our water source until it ran dry a few days later. We then discovered the hermit's spring in the forest. The water that flowed from his rusting pipe made it unnecessary to move to the mainland. Thanks, Jim.

After dinner—Top Ramen with sliced onion, canned peas, and tuna fish, with a Kit Kat for each of us for desert—we erected the small backpacking tent. We covered our duffels with a poncho and, thoroughly tired, crawled into our sleeping bags while it was still light and immediately fell asleep.

That night, and for the rest of our time in the bay, we were haunted by a grizzly bear. I can't say it was the same bear with any degree of certainty, but its near-constant presence just out of sight implied a singleness of purpose.

The spirit bear followed us around the bay, delivering messages that I could not decipher: guttural sounds, steaming piles of scat, a fresh paw mark in the sand, the pervasive odor of rotting flesh, and crushed bushes slowly rebounding from the weight of a very large supine presence.

We never saw him or her, just numerous signs from the black sand beaches to the subalpine heights. But that ursine presence was very much on our minds.

Alex carried a wooden club in his small hand everywhere he went. The only time he felt completely safe was when he stood, club in hand, upon the high steel platform that surrounded a navigational light on the shoreline of the bay.

The first contact with the bear was, for me, the most unnerving.

I awakened that night to the sound of shuffling noises and a grunt or two. And then there was the unmistakable stink of bear, a smell I was familiar with from past wilderness experiences.

I went rigid in my sleeping bag.

I debated whether to awaken Alex but decided against it. He might make a noise and startle the bear into some type of decisive action. Silence was our best and only defense. I was glad we kept no food in or near the tent. I had been adamant about that.

The cloth enclosure felt like an open crypt. I kept envisioning claws ripping razor-like through the thin green fabric as I gazed upward in mortal terror and tried to think if there was anything I could do. There wasn't.

Who could divine the thoughts of a bear, and an invisible one at that? Not I, for sure. A thousand-pound grizzly could attack either on a whim or for a very good reason that would be beyond my ability to comprehend.

What crossed my mind was our complete vulnerability to another species. I was well aware of the destructive power of our species, but to have the roles reversed was new to me.

The noises came and went; the smell was constant; then both disappeared. I had no idea how much time had elapsed.

I gulped a breath of clean, fresh air and looked forward to the possibility of an unmutilated future. It was a considerable time before I could fall asleep. There were no physical signs of the bear's presence in the morning.[†]

THE FIRST DAY was devoted to exploring our immediate environs. We decided to take the kayak and circumnavigate the island in a counterclockwise direction.

The day was cloudy. The leaden overcast cut the tops off the surrounding mountain peaks, leaving just the roots of the precipitous heights visible like so many molars, when yesterday they had been jagged incisors.

The sandy beach ended a short distance to the south, where granitic rocks intruded to form a cliff on whose ledges and fissures the kittiwakes nested. Their white bodies and light gray wings stood out against the dark cliff stained randomly by their drop-

---

[†]I later read in Stephen Herrero's book *Bear Attacks: Their Cause and Avoidance:* "Although a flimsy physical barrier, a tent may be enough of a psychological barrier to prevent the early stages of an incident, when a grizzly explores a person as something to eat. However, grizzlies have ripped tents and dragged people out and killed them. A tent only offers some protection."

pings. As we glided past, the gulls uttered their high-intensity alarm call and skittered upward, much as they had done before the 1958 earthquake.

Around the point at the southern end of the island, there was a decided change in the weather. The waves bore whitecaps and the wind contained the piercing chill of glacial heights. The kayak rocked while we put on our windbreakers.

We paddled a mile or so toward the head of the bay, and then I decided to give up attempting to make any further headway in the chop. The wind and waves, without any help from us, pushed the kayak back toward the island, and we landed on the beach that faced the head of the bay.

Alex played on the sand while I wandered to the top of a rocky promontory that promised a view. I was surprised to find a blue plastic plaque embedded in a concrete base. The weather had dulled and cracked the plastic. Scattered about the faux cenotaph were beer cans and the filter tips of cigarettes, the detritus of fishermen who had landed there to pay their respects to their fellow sailors and contemplate the expansive vista.

At the top of the plaque were inscribed the following words taken from the original cenotaph and herewith translated from the French: "At the entrance of this harbor perished twenty-one brave seamen. Reader, whoever thou art, mingle thy tears with ours." Listed under their respective ships were the names of the dead officers and crewmen. Inscribed along the bottom was "Aviso-Escorteur *Amiral Charmer*—7 Août 1978."

The French frigate *L'Amiral Charmer,* I later learned, had hove to off Lituya Bay in August of 1978 with the intent of landing a party to reestablish the cenotaph on the island. The commander surveyed the breakers at the entrance and, ever mindful of the earlier catastrophe, denied the request of his young officers to take a boat ashore. The ship sailed on to Juneau, where the plaque was given to the French vice-consul.

The next July some local history buffs chartered a boat to take the plastic cenotaph to the bay. By the time I arrived a year later, it had deteriorated badly in the harsh environment.[†]

I called to Alex to come up and see a bit of history. When I related the story behind the plaque, he said it confirmed his worst fears about the bay.

The view from the promontory, however, was marvelous. We watched the clouds swirl about the ramparts of the Fairweather Range. The weather was changing fast; the overcast was clearing. Shreds of high clouds scurried eastward. Chill shadows alternated with warm sunshine. It was truly a yin-yang landscape.

We descended to the beach, where we ambled through an open air art gallery of fanciful ice sculptures. Ice from the glaciers at the head of the bay washed ashore at high tide, and as the water receded, the rounded pieces assumed the shapes of pygmy animals, or at least they appeared so to us. Here was a small elephant, a giraffe, a kangaroo; and over there, said Alex, was a bear.

Further up on the beach was a tree trunk of truly epic proportions that had been torn from its substantial anchor in the earth by the 1958 wave. Its severed roots were spread in an umbrella shape and easily encircled my six-foot-two-inch frame.

[†] It was replaced by a bronze plaque in 1985 by the newly formed Lituya Bay Historical Society.

We got back in the kayak and continued on. At the north end of Cenotaph Island I could imagine where the French had located their observatory. But neither from water nor later on land could I find any trace of Jim Huscroft's presence on the island, other than the rusting pipe.

THE LONG SUMMER DAYS at that latitude began to blend together. Fortunately, the good weather held. Clouds and sun alternated, but there was no rain nor any unusually high winds.

I set out to explore all parts of the bay, sometimes taking Alex with me. After the two graduate students from a southern university returned to the tent I had inspected earlier, he preferred to remain behind with them. They sometimes took him fishing in their outboard-powered dory. Such a vessel was much more attractive to a teenager than a simple kayak, and he was greatly reassured by the .44-caliber Magnum revolvers strapped to their waists.[†]

I ascended Mudslide Creek and ventured into the squishy muskeg bogs beyond it, only halting at the glaciers, over which I was not equipped to walk.

From the heights above the south shore of the bay, I was on a level with the top of the opposite slope, where the vegetation had been stripped away by the giant wave. I could see the missing flank of the mountain that had slipped into the bay and the clipped-off

---

[†]I have lost their names and university affiliations. I vaguely recall that they were from a southeastern university. After that first night, I, too, was glad to have them around.

snout of the dirt-streaked Lituya Glacier that spilled out of Desolation Valley. What Miller had ascertained now made sense to me.

Early on another day, before the wind arose, Alex and I paddled to the head of Gilbert Inlet. Like Lapérouse, we were halted by the glacier and had to get out of our craft and proceed on foot. I took the precaution of hauling the kayak far above the water so that no wave from calving ice would carry it away. Had that happened, we might have been trapped there.

We climbed on the rocks along the east side of the glacier, passing a large pile of dried bear scat on the way. I wondered what a bear had been looking for so far from any food source. There were no berries or salmon in this barren place: just gray dirt, dark rocks, and glacial ice.

The arm of the glacier bent right; we followed it.

I left Alex on a level spot that did not seem prone to earthslides. I could see his freckled face and blond mop of hair as I began to climb the dirt- and boulder-strewn slope directly above the glacier. It was two steps up and one down on the crumbling slope that was poised near the angle of repose. Below, Alex nervously watched me climb and threw rocks at the fault line.

At last I reached a small niche where I could sit for a few moments with a fair degree of security. The sterile landscape was a study in various shades of gray. Nothing seemed to live upon it. Everything was poised for movement. The only regularity in the desolate scene was the arrow-straight fault.

The broken boulders, rocks, and coarse soil were the surface manifestation of colossal forces that had clashed in this place over millions of years. More than enough reasons, I thought, for the unusual history.

I descended and collected Alex, and we paddled back to the relative safety of the island.

TOGETHER, WE ALSO EXPLORED the more benign shoreline north of the bay for a distance of three miles to Echo Creek.[†] Most of the mining had taken place along this stretch of coast.

We beached the kayak in Anchorage Cove, where the climbers had established their base camp in 1958. After pulling the kayak up as high as possible, I secured it with a long line to what I hoped was a stout tree.

My greater fear for the safety of the kayak that day was bears. I thought its slick, gray rubber skin might resemble a juicy seal to those myopic beasts. I could imagine them tearing our only means of transportation to shreds, thinking it was dinner, and then their disgust and great anger when they found out otherwise.

We found the remains of the dirt road that had been hacked through the forest by gold miners. The trail passed the lake where the climbers bathed after their descent from Mount Fairweather. Lily pads floated on the surface, and two moose were knee-deep in the water, feeding on the vegetation.

Near the lake an olive-colored Army truck of World War II vintage, yet another relic of an ill-advised mining venture, was

---

[†]Maps are a good indicator of wildness. The miners knew Echo Creek as Threemile Creek. The large-scale U.S. Geological Survey topographical map calls it Fourmile Creek. On the smaller-scale USGS map, it is labeled Echo Creek. Both maps are the latest versions, and both were published forty years ago. They were drawn from aerial photographs taken in the 1940s and 1950s and were not field-checked for accuracy.

parked at a ninety-degree angle to the road. It was hard to imagine how it had gotten there, unless there had been a conscious effort to junk it.

The front end was canted upward toward the road. The rear wheels were in a ditch. It resembled a Tlingit mask. The two broken windshields were empty eye sockets, and the missing radiator was a gaping mouth.

Looking for a more pristine scene, I decided to leave the beaten path that followed the trace of the old road and cut through a thin strip of vegetation to what I hoped would be the beach. Alex followed reluctantly.

I made the move too soon and we had to boulder-hop for the next half mile through the rubble deposited by the terminal moraine. The going was tedious, but we were soon rewarded for our efforts.

We stumbled across the remains of a wrecked boat, possibly of Tlingit origin. There were two cedar fragments of what had once been a functioning vessel. I recognized the pieces as the forward decking, into which a hatch opening had been incised, and the starboard bow.

Painted on the side of the carvel-built hull was a single eye. The simple black-and-white symbol was quite distinct against the background of weathered gray wood. The eye was a motif that had also adorned Tlingit canoes and paddles. The unblinking organ followed me as I circled the remains of the wooden craft.

The day was becoming warm. We moved on. The boulders ended, and there was easier walking on the beach. Alex was getting tired. I wanted to push on beyond Portage Creek; we compromised on Echo Creek's being the end of the hike.

Just short of Echo Creek, we came upon a string of half-ruined miners' shacks set back a short distance from the beach. Inside were calendars, on which dates had been angrily crossed off, and moldering medical supplies. Matchbooks with mundane advertising on the covers and empty pints of whiskey lay scattered about. Each cabin had two rusting army cots. Bleak quarters, I thought.

Further back in the woods was a hulking piece of yellow machinery that looked as if it had been designed to rip and tear the beach sands apart in some ungodly manner. The vegetation was reclaiming it. The metallic monster had been manufactured in Ohio and was now being interred in Alaska.[†]

We ate lunch in the dune grass. I planned to take a short nap in the sun. Alex said he would like to check out the beach. I told him not to go too far and lay down. He fetched me a few minutes later.

I followed him to the wet sand near the creek, where he silently pointed to the single fresh imprint of a grizzly's paw. There was just the one signature.

[†] In a 1972 prospectus for a private stock offering, which bore a striking resemblance to the glowing report that drew the Nelsons to Lituya Bay in 1899, these structures were identified as the Lituya Placer's Camp. Gold Reserve Mining Inc., a Nevada corporation headed by Oregonians, proposed to take over the one hundred and thirty-six placer claims along the beach north of the bay and turn a net profit of $14.7 million in twenty-five years. The rising price of gold and an unspecified "technological breakthrough" were cited as reasons for the high expectations. There was no mention in the ninety-page prospectus of bad weather, bears, giant waves, or drownings at the entrance to the harbor, "which can easily be entered with barges at slack tide."

The tide might have erased the other marks, I explained lamely.

He looked at me, skeptically.

I shrugged.

We returned by a different route through the dense forest. Our periodic visitor rejoined us. The rancid smell of bear accompanied us partway. I blew the whistle often; and Alex, who normally was embarrassed by my singing, encouraged my off-key bellowing.

After crossing Portage Creek we came upon the ruins of a log cabin. It was guarded by the spiked stalks of devil's club plants, through which we carefully made our way.

Although the roof had collapsed and melted into the forest floor, the stout side walls and lintel were still upright. I entered, and amongst the wet ferns that grew inside the small enclosure lay a dented kettle on a moss-covered mound. Its lid was missing.

Incredible, I thought. The small kettle must have been used to heat water for tea. The first person who came to mind was the Englishwoman Hannah Nelson.

I imagined that this dank place was the Nelsons' cabin, where the killing took place and the murderer was subdued. I later learned that it had been one of Huscroft's trapping cabins, but that did not rule out its having been someone else's cabin before Huscroft's arrival in the bay. It could also have been the cabin where the murderer was guarded by the Indians. There was no certainty in this and other matters pertaining to the bay.

We completed the hike; the kayak was unharmed.

ON ANOTHER DAY I ventured alone toward the mouth of the bay. I would not have taken Alex anywhere near that entrance, even if he had wanted to accompany me, which he didn't. The two researchers said he could go fishing with them. Alex was pleased.

I took no chances, although I was going to paddle no closer than one mile to the entrance. I carefully timed my departure to coincide with the start of the flood current and landed near Anchorage Cove.

I cut left and walked out onto the spit at approximately the point where Severts had died with a rope around his neck. The hanging tree, and all others on the spit, had been swept away by subsequent giant waves.

A steaming mound of bear shit, liberally laced with undigested berries, lay directly in my path. Now, there was a statement.

The bent limbs of bushes, where a large object had just been resting, rose slowly from their horizontal position, as if propelled upward by a ghost-like presence. I looked about me but saw and smelled nothing.

I walked along the rock-lined spit that Lapérouse had thought resembled a harbor mole and sat at the end, perhaps in the same spot where the Tlingit woman had mourned the loss of her eight brothers with songs.

The fiberglass wreckage of the *Sonora Sue* was stuck in the rocks. A departing fishing boat bucked the incoming swells with little difficulty.

ON THE SEVENTH DAY I ventured forth on my last excursion. This time I headed toward Harbor Point on the south side of the entrance. I took the same precautions as before, making sure that I departed on the incoming current.

I landed near where the Tlingit village and graveyard had

been located. I could find no evidence of the departed Indians after a brief search.

In a light rain, which increased the slipperiness of the round boulders, I made my way to the point. What if I fell, jammed my ankle, and broke a leg? My thoughts had been full of such worst-case scenarios during my time in the bay.

I took shelter near Cormorant Rock and watched the considerable amount of airplane traffic flying both ways on this day of reduced visibility. The planes, whose pilots were flying a visual flight plan, were indistinct shapes a few hundred yards off the entrance.

There are some who believe the plane carrying Hale Boggs of Louisiana, majority leader of the U.S. House of Representatives, dropped out of the sky near here and disappeared, altering national politics for a short period of time.

The weather had also been poor on October 16th, 1972, when Boggs and an Alaskan congressman and his aide left Anchorage in a twin-engine plane flown by an experienced Alaskan bush pilot. Juneau was their destination. Twelve minutes into the trip the pilot radioed his visual flight plan. It would have taken him over the entrance to Lituya Bay. Nothing further was heard, although the plane was equipped with an emergency transmitting device.

The most extensive land and sea search in Alaska's short history was launched by all the relevant military forces, civil agencies, and civilian volunteers. It centered around the Portage Pass area south of Anchorage and in and around the Lituya Bay region. Sheila Nickerson, a Juneau resident and author of *Disappearance: A Map,* wrote: "In spite of a massive search . . . no sign of the plane was ever found. From psychics to spy planes, from dreams to heat-sensing detectors, every possible method was used."[†]

I wondered if it was still possible for a sign to be flashed by the bear slaves atop the Fairweather Range and for Kah Lituya, the monster of the deep, to reach up and just snatch that plane from the sky.

I returned to the island. Alex and I flew, as prearranged, to Juneau the next day; but not before we had our final thumb-wrestling match for the championship of Lituya Bay and, more important, for first use of the shower in the hotel room.

I won, but I let him go first. What else could the relieved father of a son like that do?

Looking back from the vantage point of twenty years, and with far greater knowledge of that place than I possessed at the time, taking Alex with me now seems like a grave mistake. Releasing Alex unharmed was the greatest gift the bay could give me.

ALEX FLEW HOME the next day to a long summer vacation filled with all the earthly delights that only California can offer a teen-ager. I plunged into further research on the bay at the Alaska State Library in Juneau.

I came across a newspaper clipping stating that Bill Swanson had died in Lituya Bay. I somehow knew there was more to the story than just that simple fact. I went to the Bureau of Vital Statistics where, not being a relative, I had to cajole the clerk into giving me more precise information on the manner and timing

---

[†]Nickerson's book on death and loss throughout the state begins: "I live in a place where people disappear. Alaska. Too large to comprehend."

of his death. The details emerged, to be collaborated later by Vi Swanson. More than coincidence seemed to be involved in his death.

I returned to my hotel, badly shaken. The more I learned, the more fearful I became of that bay and its fatal legacy, which now seemed to be reaching out for me. In retrospect, there appear to be four reasons for my acute sensitivity to Lituya Bay, although I have talked to others who have felt similarly, for different reasons, about other wild places.

As a journalist in the 1960s, I had specialized in violence. I chased urban conflicts and foreign wars and felt immune to harm. In the next decade I encountered the bay while I was in my mid-forties, a more vulnerable time. By then I had a growing awareness of my mortality.

My subsequent visit to the outermost island of Attu and the remaining evidence—such as barracks, shell holes, and unexploded ordnance—of many violent deaths during World War II did not help to calm me. I was suffering from a surfeit of death.

I am susceptible to the suggestive powers of both human and natural history. I once assumed the symptoms of the cancer victims I described in another book; fortunately, they were benign. When the usual fall rains fail to arrive on time in California to end the months of drought, I become very nervous.

And lastly, there is the unconscious. Our feelings about a place, and its impact on us, derive from many factors in our past. The whiplash of my mother's erratic moods, and thus the rhythm of my early years, matched the vicissitudes of Lituya Bay, which is why it assumed a feminine presence for me.

It was a dark and confusing time in my life.

$\mathcal{T}$OMALES $\mathcal{B}$AY.

———

AFTER RETURNING FROM ALASKA I set off to visit the two widowed women who might be able to tell me something about the bay. Although I was a stranger who came knocking on their doors with an unusual request—to speak of Lituya Bay and the deaths of their husbands two decades earlier—they confided things to me that they had not divulged to others. There was an instant rapport between us.

I visited Vi Swanson first. I remember the bric-a-brac in her mobile home near Seattle and its tidiness. She was certain there had been a white light on shore. The white-haired Mrs. Swanson drew my attention to the names of the two boats that had heard the calls for help, the *Lumen* and the *White Light.* Yes, she said, her hair had turned color that night.

She gave me something cold to drink and engaged me in conversation overlong. I had the impression that she was lonely. But there was more to it than that. I thanked her and left. She later wrote me from a rest home. It was a feisty letter, full of life.

Before visiting Carmel Miller, I went looking for traces of her husband at the regional office of the U.S. Geological Survey in Menlo Park. I read Miller's handwritten field notes; it was like touching the man. Then I visited with George Plafker, one of Miller's colleagues and an authority on the Fairweather Fault.

Plafker mentioned that Miller's wife had changed, had become different in some way. I called her, and she said she would talk to me. I drove into San Francisco on a hot fall day. The family home was in the Sunset District, close to the ocean.

Carmel Miller offered me lemonade, and we sat in the kitchen. Books were stacked all about on shelves, tables, and the floor of the living room and kitchen. I noticed Carlos Castaneda titles and some works on parapsychology. She had gone back to school, she said, to get a graduate degree; she was seeking something. So was I.

Mrs. Miller said it was the first time she had spoken of her husband to anyone since his death. He had been awed by the raw power of the giant waves and the fact that he had been nearby when the 1958 wave struck. Miller frequently mentioned the seeming coincidence to his wife.

He was a tense man, a complex man. He loved his family but needed to get away to Alaska for months at a time each year. Mrs. Miller thought that it was odd that he had drowned near where he had begun his career with the geological survey twenty years earlier. They had also been married for twenty years, she noted.

She took me down to the basement, where Miller's home office had been kept intact as a shrine to his memory.

There was a print of a glacier-fed Alaskan river above his desk. It had been his favorite—a somber, dark representation of Alaska. When she looked at it, Mrs. Miller said, she got the impression it was underwater.

I thought the painting depicted the place where Miller had drowned.

I began to sweat in the cool basement.

Mrs. Miller was reaching back, and I knew what was coming.

"I often wondered if he was flirting with death. There is something tremendously thrilling about that. It was an ominous place, and the sense of destruction was so great."

I felt that she was talking about *me*.

A HEAVY DARKNESS had settled over the small communities surrounding Tomales Bay shortly after my return from Alaska. Violence was abroad in the form of an armed cult and a serial killer who preyed upon women. At the same time, a local youth stole into our homes and took food, baubles, and mementos. I felt responsible. I thought some essence of Lituya Bay had come trailing after me and spread across the watershed in which I lived.

At the height of the communal hysteria and fear, I saw what I thought was a Land Otter Man.

Day-Glo orange signs posted by the Park Service warned hikers not to walk alone, but I ventured forth. I wanted to reclaim what I thought was rightfully mine—the ability to seek solace alone in the wilderness.

I was walking along Inverness Ridge in the Point Reyes National Seashore, where the coastal landscape closely resembles the Alaskan rain forest. The dense stand of Douglas firs on Sky Trail blocked the light, fog swirled through the trees, and the ferns dripped moisture. The day was warm, and I sweated as I made my way up a slight incline.

Another lone man was walking toward me. He was swathed in wool from head to toe: tweed cap, tweed sports coat, flannel slacks, and a long, wool scarf wrapped around his neck. The man-beast had the pointed, hairy face of an otter, a species I was familiar with.

I can still view the Land Otter Man on the screen inside my mind. I have subsequently walked past that exact spot in better times and seen nothing unusual.

THERE WAS ONE last place to visit. The American Museum of Natural History in New York City possessed the greatest number of Tlingit artifacts, most having been collected by George Emmons.

My wife, Dianne, accompanied me. Like Alex, she was companion, shield, and litmus test.

I had written ahead explaining my purpose. In reply, I was told that we should present ourselves at the information desk, where we would be directed to Anibal Rodriguez, a curator who specialized in Tlingit matters.

We wandered through the Northwest Hall before making our presence known. The somberness of the Tlingits permeated this darkened region of the museum.

Dianne did not find the Tlingits to be life affirming, like the Navajo or Hopi of the Southwest. "Heavy and dark," she said as we walked slowly past leering masks in wood and glass cases and howling creatures perched atop totem poles.

The hall was virtually unchanged since a 1943 photograph that appeared in Claude Lévi-Strauss's book *The Way of the Masks*. The anthropologist wrote: "The masks' primal message retains so much power that even today the prophylactic insulation of the showcases fails to muffle its communication." The impact had not lessened during the intervening forty-five years.

We found Rodriguez amidst the clutter of the Junius Bird Laboratory of South American Archaeology. He asked what I was after, and I explained my purpose. I wanted to examine and touch some Tlingit artifacts in the hope that they might give me insight. Rodriguez, a man of slight frame, medium height, and dark hair, was polite but guarded.

We followed him through the maze of hallways and past a diorama of archeological artifacts from around the world. Proceeding up steel stairs, we passed Margaret Mead's old office. We stopped at Room 23 on the sixth floor, and Rodriguez unlocked and unbolted the steel door. It creaked open. The small room smelled like a musty, disused closet.

There were rows upon rows of artifacts in boxes or sitting loose on steel-mesh shelves. They hung from pipes and electrical conduits along the sides and ceiling of the room. The profusion of articles and the juxtaposition of solid forms and primary colors made for a turbulent scene.

My wife and the curator waited at the door while I stepped into the room. I pushed the red button on the tape recorder and spoke. My words echoed off the cold walls. As I listen to the recording now, I hear my short, rapid breaths between words:

The contorted faces. The nose that winds into the mouth. The long beaks. One face green, red mouth gaping, bulging black eyes. The eyes, always the eyes. I touch the wooden armor and the dust comes off on the sweat of my hands. Snares, the intricacy of the bird traps. I am putting my hands on a trap. A pair of what looks like baby boots. How can anyone from my culture really understand what is being said here.

After standing motionless and silent in the storage room for some minutes, I turned and walked back into the hallway and present time.

Rodriguez had listened carefully to my soliloquy. Apparently he liked what he had heard, because he was immediately more forthcoming. I had passed some kind of test.

He asked, "Is it the mask or is it you? When you approach something on the shelf and you see the dead-looking, deep eyes and you know it's shamanistic, you wonder: are you reacting to your childhood fears, is there a scientific explanation, a psychological reason, or is it cultural? How do you reconcile these feelings? I don't know. All I can say is that it happens, and I think along the way there is an opportunity for you to figure it out, if you want to figure it out."

I said I was trying to figure it out by writing a book.

"Yes," Rodriguez replied, "and I think it depends on the individual who is writing the book as to how much of yourself, how much of your beliefs, how much of your superstitions, and how much of your fears go into it."

"What about the power of place?" I asked, thinking of Lituya Bay. "For instance, what happens to you when you go into that room looking for, say, specimen number x2754? What does that room, or any place for that matter, do to you that is not conscious?"

"I think it's mood," he said, "I think there is an environment here. Some places will give you an eerie feeling. For example, I know that this is an old place. I know it has a long and valued history, and there are a lot of characters involved in that history. There are a lot of stories that go with these names. There's a big difference when you look at an object in this room and when you go to a modern state-of-the-art storage room. When you walk into a bright, well-lit, air-conditioned room, it does something else to your senses."

"You're not even aware of it," Dianne said. "It's on a subliminal level."

"Very subliminal," said Rodriguez. "I have been around here long enough that I've been able to compare notes, so to speak."

He motioned toward the open steel door: "This room has a special quality, a built-in quality. It is crowded, it is overwhelming, and it's not organized. There's something interesting, something attractive about disorganization, because it reflects history. Things come in slowly, and they accumulate, and you see objects as they appear intermittently in succession. By just arriving they tell a story, or want to tell a story. We don't know exactly what that story is, but we *feel* something. Something is going on."

I thought he could easily be talking about the accumulation of facts and impressions that constituted the history of Lituya Bay and my reaction to it. Like Castaneda, perhaps I had found my insightful shaman.

I asked Dianne to take a photograph of me in front of Room 23, with and without a Tlingit mask affixed to my face.

And there I am: gaunt, serious face above a dark blue blazer, and then the shaman's mask with the tufts of hair, black holes for eyes, and open mouth. Both figures wear a name tag identifying me as a visitor.

We descended the stairs, thanked Rodriguez, and left the museum.

I had lived history, and it had not been easy. I had only one conclusion: it was the experience that counted. I found that thought to be quietly satisfying.

ACKNOWLEDGMENTS.

This book represents a twenty-five-year effort to assemble my thoughts about Lituya Bay in a coherent manner and to find a publisher. I sometimes wondered if it was worth the effort, but I felt compelled to come to terms with that place through the written word.

Some people helped me along the way.

Doris Ober, to whom this book is dedicated, is a close friend and my first professional reader. For the past ten years she has read almost everything I have written and commented wisely on it. I listen closely to what she has to say.

My wife, Dianne, has been with me for two-thirds of this journey. She is a voracious reader, but this is not her kind of book. Nevertheless, she read each revision of the manuscript—and there were many—and showed me how an intelligent, albeit loyal, reader might react.

Alex Fradkin, my son, now in his thirties, is a talented photographer who would like to return to the bay with his cameras. He is welcome to do so, without me. He was a wonderful companion on that first and last trip.

One incarnation of this manuscript was fictional, and I received a small grant from the Marin Arts Council for that effort. A juror, Betty Hodson, took the time to write a letter of encouragement that kept me going for a while.

Connie Mery translated portions of works about Lapérouse that had been written in French. She and her husband, Michael, and another literate friend, Richard B. Lyttle, read earlier versions of the manuscript and helped me with their comments.

Malcolm Margolin, the only other person I know who is familiar with Lapérouse, saw value in a draft and suggested that the manuscript might find a home with a university press. When the University of California Press needed a second peer reviewer of the manuscript, he replied with intelligence and wit.

Monica McCormick, history editor for the Press, said with enthusiasm that she would like to publish the manuscript. She is a thoughtful and incisive editor. At the tail end of this prolonged effort, Dore Brown, senior project editor for the Press, enhanced my intent with perceptive copyediting.

S OURCES.

The principal repositories for information on Lituya Bay are, from south to north: the Huntington Library in Pasadena, the U.S. Geological Survey library in Menlo Park, the Bancroft Library in Berkeley, the special collections section of the University of Washington Library in Seattle, the Alaska State Library in Juneau, and the library and files of Glacier Bay National Park.

All my written notes, photocopies of research materials, and photographs were destroyed in a 1988 fire. Some were reconstructed from a computer disk stored elsewhere. Most of the research was gathered a second time. I had to rely on memory for a few incidents.

Lapérouse and Miller have made the most noteworthy contributions to the specific history of Lituya Bay. Bohn, de Laguna, Caldwell, and Nickerson have added broader and more recent strokes.

I have arranged the citations in the order of their first sustained use. Some were employed elsewhere. I have kept references to works used as background to a minimum and have not included materials that were only marginally helpful.

I. BEGINNINGS

Philip L. Fradkin. *Wanderings of an Environmental Journalist: In Alaska and the American West.* Albuquerque: University of New Mexico Press, 1993.

Dave Bohn. *Glacier Bay.* Gustavus: Alaska National Parks and Monuments Association, 1967.

Don Tocher. "The Alaska Earthquake of July 10, 1958: Movement on the Fairweather Fault and Field Investigation of Southern Epicentral Region." *Bulletin of the Seismological Society of America,* April 1960.

Ron Redfern. *The Making of a Continent.* New York: Times Books, 1986.

II. THE PLACE

Coast and Geodetic Survey. *U.S. Coast Pilot, Southeast Alaska, Dixon Entrance to Yakutat Bay.* Washington, D.C.: U.S. Government Printing Office, 1952.

Defense Mapping Agency. *Sailing Directions for the North Pacific Ocean.* 3d ed. Washington, D.C.: U.S. Government Printing Office, 1989.

Howell Williams, ed. *Landscapes of Alaska.* Berkeley: University of California Press, 1958.

Ivan Doig. *The Sea Runners.* New York: Penguin Books, 1983.

National Park Service, Gregory P. Streveler et al. *Lituya Bay Environmental Study.* Juneau, 1980.

National Park Service. *General Management Plan.* Glacier Bay National Park and Preserve, Gustavus, Alaska, 1984.

National Park Service. *Final Environmental Impact Statement for the Wilderness Recommendations.* Glacier Bay National Park and Preserve, Gustavus, Alaska, 1988.

National Park Service. *Proceedings of the Second Glacier Bay Science Symposium.* Glacier Bay National Park and Preserve, Gustavus, Alaska, 1988.

III. THE TLINGITS

George E. Marcus and Michael M. J. Fischer. *Anthropology as Cultural Critique.* Chicago: University of Chicago Press, 1986.

Clifford Geertz. *The Interpretation of Cultures.* New York: Basic Books, 1973.

James Clifford and George E. Marcus, eds. *Writing Culture: The Poetics and Politics of Ethnography.* Berkeley: University of California Press, 1986.

A. J. Jaffe. *The First Immigrants from Asia: A Population History of the North American Indians.* New York: Plenum Press, 1992.

Jesse D. Jennings, ed. *Ancient Native Americans.* San Francisco: W. H. Freeman, 1978.

Brian M. Fagan. *The Great Journey: The Peopling of Ancient America.* New York: Thames and Hudson, 1987.

Frederica de Laguna. *Under Mount Saint Elias: The History and Culture of the Yakutat Tlingit.* 3 vols. Washington, D.C.: Smithsonian Institution Press, 1972.

Aurel Krause. *The Tlingit Indians.* Seattle: University of Washington Press, 1956.

Archimandrite Anatoli Kamenskii. *Tlingit Indians of Alaska.* Fairbanks: University of Alaska Press, 1985.

Aldona Jonaitis. *Art of the Northern Tlingits.* Seattle: University of Washington Press, 1986.

John R. Swanton. *Social Conditions, Beliefs, and Linguistic Relationship of the Tlingit Indians.* Bureau of American Ethnology, 26th Annual Report. Washington, D.C.: Smithsonian Institution Press, 1908.

John R. Swanton. *Tlingit Myths and Texts.* Bureau of American Ethnology, Bulletin 39. Washington, D.C.: Smithsonian Institution Press, 1909.

R. L. Olson. *Social Structure and Social Life of the Tlingit in Alaska.* Berkeley: University of California Press, 1967.

Kalervo Oberg. *The Social Economy of the Tlingit Indians.* Seattle: University of Washington Press, 1973.

Walter R. Goldschmidt and Theodore H. Haas. *Possessory Rights of the Natives of Southeastern Alaska.* A Report to the Commissioner of Indian Affairs. 1946.

Livingston F. Jones. *A Study of the Tlingits of Alaska.* New York: Fleming H. Revell, 1914.

Nora Marks Dauenhauer and Richard Dauenhauer, eds. *Haa Shuká, Our Ancestors.* Seattle: University of Washington Press, 1987.

Claude Lévi-Strauss. *The Way of the Masks.* Translated by Sylvia Modelski. Seattle: University of Washington Press, 1988.

Alec Wilkinson. "The Uncommitted Crime." *The New Yorker,* November 26, 1990.

IV. THE FRENCH

F. A. Golder. *Russian Expansion on the Pacific, 1641–1850.* Cleveland: Arthur H. Clark, 1914.

F. A. Golder. *Bering's Voyages.* 2 vols. New York: American Geographical Society, 1922.

Vasilii A. Divin. *The Great Russian Navigator A. I. Chirikov.* Fairbanks: University of Alaska Press, 1993.

Glynn Barratt. *Russia in Pacific Waters, 1715–1825.* Vancouver: University of British Columbia Press, 1981.

Hubert Howe Bancroft. *History of Alaska.* San Francisco: A. L. Bancroft, 1886.

William Coxe. *Account of the Russian Discoveries between Asia and America.* London: Cadell and Davies, 1804.

Raymond H. Fisher. *Bering's Voyages: Whither and Why.* Seattle: University of Washington Press, 1977.

J. C. Beaglehole. *The Voyage of the* Resolution *and* Discovery, *1776–1780.* Vol. 3. London: Hakluyt Society, 1967.

J. C. Beaglehole. *The Life of Captain James Cook.* London: Hakluyt Society, 1974.

Stephen Haycox et al., eds. *Enlightenment and Exploration in the North Pacific, 1741–1805.* Seattle: University of Washington Press, 1997.

George Thornton Emmons. "Native Account of the Meeting between La Pérouse and the Tlingit." *American Anthropology* 13 (April–June 1911).

Jean-François de Galaup de la Pérouse. *The Journal of Jean-François de Galaup de la Pérouse.* Vols. 1–2. Translated and edited by John Dunmore. London: Hakluyt Society, 1994.

Jean François de Lapérouse. *A Voyage 'Round the World, 1785–1788.* London: Lackington, Allen, 1807.

Julius S. Gassner. *Voyages and Adventures of La Pérouse.* Honolulu: University of Hawaii Press, 1969.

John Dunmore. *Pacific Explorer: The Life of Jean-François de Galaup de la Pérouse (1741–1788).* Annapolis, Md.: Naval Institute Press, 1985.

François Bellec. *La généreuse et tragique expédition Lapérouse.* Rennes: Ouest-France, 1985.

Edward Weber Allen. *The Vanishing Frenchman: The Mysterious Disappearance of Lapérouse.* Rutland, Vt.: C. E. Tuttle, 1959.

Russell C. Shelton. *From Hudson Bay to Botany Bay: The Lost Frigates of Lapérouse.* Toronto: NC Press, 1987.

Simon Schama. *Citizens.* New York: Vintage Books, 1990.

Oliver Bernier. *Louis the Beloved: The Life of Louis XV.* Garden City, N.Y.: Doubleday, 1984.

Malcolm Margolin. *Monterey in 1786: The Journals of Jean François de La Pérouse.* Berkeley: Heyday Books, 1989.

Jean Baptiste Barthélemy de Lesseps. *Travels in Kamchatka during the Years 1787 and 1788.* London: J. Johnson, St. Paul's Church Yard, 1790.

Jacques Julien Houton de Labillardière. *An Account of a Voyage in Search of La Pérouse Undertaken by Order of the Constituent Assembly of France and Performed in the Years 1791, 1792, and 1793 in the* Recherche *and* Esperance, *Ships of War, Under the Command of Rear-Admiral Bruny d'Entrécasteaux.* 2d ed. London: B. Uphill, 1802.

Peter Dillon. *Narrative and Successful Result of a Voyage in the South Seas Performed by Order of the Government of British India to Ascertain the Actual Fate of La Pérouse's Expedition, Interspersed with Accounts of the Religion, Manners, Customs, and Cannibal Practices of the South Sea Islanders.* London: Hurst, Chance, 1829.

James W. Davidson. *Peter Dillon of Vanikoro.* New York: Oxford University Press, 1975.

V. THE RUSSIANS

Grigorii I. Shelikhov. *A Voyage to America, 1783–1786.* Kingston, Ontario: Limestone Press, 1981.

A. I. Andreyev, ed. *Russian Discoveries in the Pacific and in North America in the Eighteenth and Nineteenth Centuries.* American Council of Learned Societies, 1952.

P. A. Tikhmenev. *A History of the Russian-American Company.* Seattle: University of Washington Press, 1978.

Frederic W. Horway, ed. *Voyages of the* Columbia *to the Northwest Coast, 1787–1790 and 1790–1793.* Oregon Historical Society, 1990.

Kalervo Okerg. *The Social Economy of the Tlingit Indians.* Seattle: University of Washington Press, 1973.

Erna Gunther. *Indian Life on the Northwest Coast of America.* Chicago: University of Chicago Press, 1972.

Henry W. Elliott. *An Arctic Province.* London: Sampson et al., 1886.

William H. Dall. *Alaska and Its Resources.* Boston: Lee and Shepard, 1897.

VI. THE AMERICANS

U.S. Coast and Geodetic Survey and George Davidson. *Coast Pilot of Alaska.* 1st ed. Washington, D.C.: U.S. Government Printing Office, 1869.

George Davidson. "Scientific Expedition to Alaska." *Harper's Monthly,* November 1868.

U.S. House of Representatives. 44th Cong., 1st sess. *Report of the Superintendent of the U.S. Coast Survey, Showing Progress of the Survey During the Year 1875.* Washington, D.C.: U.S. Government Printing Office, 1878.

U.S. Coast and Geodetic Survey and W. H. Dall. *Pacific Coast Pilot.* 2d ed. Part 1. Washington, D.C.: U.S. Government Printing Office, 1883.

Otto J. Klotz. "Notes on Glaciers of South-Eastern Alaska and Adjoining Territory." *Geographical Journal,* 1899.

W. H. Dall. "Alaska As It Is and Was." Washington, D.C.: Philosophical Society of Washington, December 6, 1895.

Edward A. Herron. *First Scientist of Alaska: William Healey Dall.* New York: Julian Messner, 1958.

U.S. Geological Survey and Donald J. Orth. *Dictionary of Alaska Place Names.* USGS Professional Paper 567. Washington, D.C.: U.S. Government Printing Office, 1967.

U.S. Coast and Geodetic Survey and Lt. Cmdr. Henry E. Nichols. *Pacific Coast Pilot, Alaska.* 3d ed. Part 1. Washington, D.C.: U.S. Government Printing Office, 1891.

Jean Low. "George Thornton Emmons." *Alaska Journal,* Winter 1977.

George Thornton Emmons. *The Tlingit Indians.* Edited by Frederica de Laguna. Seattle: University of Washington Press, 1991.

Douglas Cole. *Captured Heritage: The Scramble for Northwest Coast Artifacts.* Seattle: University of Washington Press, 1985.

Aldona Jonaitis. *From the Land of the Totem Poles.* New York: American Museum of Natural History, 1988.

U.S. Geological Survey and J. B. Mertie Jr. *Notes on the Geography and Geology of Lituya Bay, Alaska.* Bulletin 863-B. Washington, D.C.: U.S. Government Printing Office, 1931.

U.S. Geological Survey, Erk Reimnitz and George Plafker. *Marine Gold Placers along the Gulf of Alaska Margin.* Bulletin 1415. Washington, D.C.: U.S. Government Printing Office, 1976.

C. Perry McBeth. "Gold at Lituya." *Alaska Sportsman,* February 1949.

John Burroughs, John Muir, and George Bird Grinnell. *Alaska.* Vol. 1. Harriman Alaska Expedition. New York: Doubleday, Page, 1901.

George Bird Grinnell. *Alaska 1899: Essays from the Harriman Expedition.* Seattle: University of Washington Press, 1995.

Grove Karl Gilbert. *Glaciers and Glaciation*. Harriman Alaska Series. Vol. 3. Washington, D.C.: Smithsonian Institution, 1910.

Linnie Marsh Wolfe, ed. *John of the Mountains*. Madison: University of Wisconsin Press, 1979.

Nancy Lord. *Green Alaska*. Washington, D.C.: Counterpoint, 1999.

Herman J. Viola. *Exploring the West*. Washington, D.C.: Smithsonian Books, 1987.

William H. Goertzmann and Kay Sloan. *Looking Far North: The Harriman Expedition to Alaska, 1899.* New York: Viking Press, 1982.

U.S. Geological Survey, Ralph S. Tarr, and Lawrence Martin. *The Earthquakes at Yakutat Bay, Alaska, in September, 1899.* USGS Professional Paper 69. Washington, D.C.: U.S. Government Printing Office, 1912.

"Prospectus of the Latuya Bay Gold Mining Company." Latuya Bay Gold Mining Company. San Francisco, 1899.

The [Sitka] Alaskan, May 12, 1900, and October 13, 1906.

"Woman Hangs a Man And the Law Upholds Her." *San Francisco Examiner,* October 14, 1900.

Jack London. "The Unexpected." *McClure's,* August 1906.

Franklin Walker. *Jack London and the Klondike*. San Marino, Calif.: Huntington Library, 1994.

Earle Labor, ed. *The Letters of Jack London*. Vol. 2, *1906–1912.* Stanford: Stanford University Press, 1988.

William R. Hunt. *Distant Justice: Policing the Alaskan Frontier*. Norman: University of Oklahoma Press, 1987.

Merle Colby. *A Guide to Alaska, Last American Frontier*. New York: Macmillan, 1939.

Francis E. Caldwell. *Land of the Ocean Mists*. Edmonds: Alaska Northwest Publishing, 1986.

Allen Carpe. "The Conquest of Mt. Fairweather." *Alpine Journal,* November 1931.

H. Bradford Washburn Jr. *The Harvard-Dartmouth Alaskan Expeditions*. Geographical Journal, June 1936.

Bradford Washburn. "The Conquest of Mount Crillon." *National Geographic,* March 1935.

Dave Bohn. "Portrait of an Expedition in the Fairweather Range." *American Alpine Journal,* 1963.

Arthur Mallory. "Lituya's Elusive Gold." *Alaska Sportsman,* August 1964.

Jay Williams. "Lituya Bay, the Bewitcher." *Alaska Sportsman,* February 1938.

Jay Williams. *Alaskan Adventure.* Harrisburg, Pa.: Stackpole, 1952.

VII. THE WAVE

Donald J. Miller. *Giant Waves in Lituya Bay, Alaska.* USGS Professional Paper 354-C. Washington, D.C.: U.S. Government Printing Office, 1960.

Don Tocher and Don J. Miller et al. "The Alaska Earthquake of July 10, 1958." *Bulletin of the Seismological Society of America,* April 1960.

Don J. Miller. "Cataclysmic Flood Waves in Lituya Bay, Alaska." *Bulletin of the Seismological Society of America,* July 1954.

Don Tocher and Don J. Miller. "Field Observation on Effects of Alaska Earthquake of 10 July 1958." *Science,* February 13, 1959.

R. J. Brazee and James N. Jordan. "Preliminary Notes of Southeastern Alaska Earthquake." *Earthquake Notes,* Seismological Society of America, September 1958.

Don Tocher, ed. "Seismological Notes." *Seismological Society of America Bulletin,* October 1958.

Don J. Miller, Thomas G. Payne, and George Gryc. *Geology of Possible Petroleum Provinces in Alaska.* Geological Survey Bulletin 1094. Washington, D.C.: U.S. Government Printing Office, 1959.

G. F. Jordan. "Redistribution of Sediments in Alaskan Bays and Inlets." *Geographical Review* (New York), 1962.

Paddy Sherman. *Cloud Walkers: Six Climbs on Major Canadian Peaks.* New York: St. Martin's Press, 1965.

Transcript of the radio interview with Bill Swanson and Diane Olson's notes on the radio transmissions, Glacier Bay National Park files, Juneau.

Howard Ulrich. "Night of Terror." *Alaska Sportsman,* October 1958.

Bill Swanson. "Where Hell Breaks Loose." *Alaska Sportsman,* October 1958.

K. E. Hilmar. "The Hand That Rocks the Earth: Earthquake at Sea." *Oceans,* July–August 1978.

Lawrence Elliott. "There's a Tidal Wave Loose in There." *Reader's Digest,* July 1960.

Elliott Roberts. "The Day the Bay Ran Over." *U.S. Naval Institute Proceedings,* May 1960.

California Division of Mines and Geology, Mineral Information Service. *The Biggest Splash in History.* December 1965.

Hisashi Miyoshi. "Notes on the Highest Waves in History." *Jishin* (Seismological Society of Japan newsletter) 25, no. 24 (1972).

Robert L. Wiegel. *Oceanographical Engineering.* Englewood Cliffs, N.J.: Prentice-Hall, 1964.

M. J. Tucker. *Waves in Ocean Engineering.* London: Ellis Horwood, 1991.

Robert E. Ackerman. "The Archeology of the Glacier Bay Region, Southeastern Alaska." Washington State University, Laboratory of Anthropology, report no. 44 (1968).

VIII. THE PRESENT

Jeff Rennicke. *Bears of Alaska in Life and Legend.* Boulder, Colo.: Roberts Rinehart, 1987.

Stephen Herrero. *Bear Attacks: Their Causes and Avoidance.* New York: Nick Lyons Books, 1985.

Thomas McNamee. *The Grizzly Bear.* New York: McGraw-Hill, 1986.

Roderick Nash. *Wilderness and the American Mind.* New Haven: Yale University Press, 1982.

Theodore Catton. *Land Reborn: A History of Administration and Visitor Use in Glacier Bay National Park and Preserve.* Anchorage: National Park Service, 1995.

Theodore Catton. *Inhabited Wilderness: Indian, Eskimos, and National Parks in Alaska.* Albuquerque: University of New Mexico Press, 1997.

"Glacier Bay: A Guide to Glacier Bay National Park and Preserve." Washington, D.C.: National Park Service, 1983.

"Development Plan for Lituya Bay Beach Deposits." Vancouver, Wash.: Gold Reserve Mining, Inc., January 2, 1972.

Sheila Nickerson. *Disappearance: A Map.* New York: Doubleday, 1996.

U.S. Congress, Joint Committee on Printing. *Memorial Services, Hale Boggs.* Washington, D.C.: U.S. Government Printing Office, 1973.

IX. TOMALES BAY

Anibal Rodriguez Jr., American Museum of Natural History, New York City, October 23, 1989.

INDEX.

Note: Italicized page numbers indicate maps and photographs.

Designer: Nola Burger
Text: 11/15 Granjon
Display: Granjon; Centaur Swash
Compositor: G&S Typesetters, Inc.
Printer and binder: Maple-Vail Manufacturing Group